SCIENCE
FUSION

fusion [FYOO • zhuhn] a combination of two or more things that releases energy

---

This Write-In Student Edition belongs to

_____

Teacher/Room

_____

 HOUGHTON MIFFLIN HARCOURT

HOUGHTON MIFFLIN HARCOURT

Front Cover: *turtle* ©Westend6l GmbH/Alamy; *bubbles* ©Andrew Holt/Alamy; *guitar* ©Brand Z/Alamy; *giraffe* ©Nicholas Eveleigh/Stockbyte/Getty Images; *observatory* ©Robert Llewellyn/Workbook Stock/Getty Images; *wind turbine* ©Comstock/Getty Images

Back Cover: *prism* ©Larry Lilac/Alamy; *clownfish* ©Georgette Douwma/Photographer's Choice/Getty Images; *galaxy* ©Stocktrek/Corbis; *fern* ©Mauro Fermariello/Photo Researchers, Inc.

Consulting Authors

Michael A. DiSpezio
Global Educator
North Falmouth, Massachusetts

Marjorie Frank
*Science Writer and Content-Area Reading
   Specialist*
Brooklyn, New York

Michael Heithaus
Director, School of Environment and Society
*Associate Professor, Department of Biological
   Sciences*
Florida International University
North Miami, Florida

Donna Ogle
Professor of Reading and Language
National-Louis University
Chicago, Illinois

Program Advisors

Paul D. Asimow
*Professor of Geology and
   Geochemistry*
California Institute of Technology
Pasadena, California

Bobby Jeanpierre
*Associate Professor of Science
   Education*
University of Central Florida
Orlando, Florida

Gerald H. Krockover
*Professor of Earth and Atmospheric
   Science Education*
Purdue University
West Lafayette, Indiana

Rose Pringle
Associate Professor
School of Teaching and Learning
College of Education
University of Florida
Gainesville, Florida

Carolyn Staudt
Curriculum Designer for Technology
KidSolve, Inc.
The Concord Consortium
Concord, Massachusetts

Larry Stookey
Science Department
Antigo High School
Antigo, Wisconsin

Carol J. Valenta
*Associate Director of the Museum and
   Senior Vice President*
Saint Louis Science Center
St. Louis, Missouri

Barry A. Van Deman
President and CEO
Museum of Life and Science
Durham, North Carolina

Power up with Science Fusion!

Your program fuses...

e-Learning & Virtual Labs

Labs & Activities

Write-In Student Edition

... to generate new science energy for today's science learner— **you.**

STEM activities throughout the program!

Write-In Student Edition

Be an active reader and make this book your own!

Food for Th...

Food is an important need for ani... ...umans. Food helps animals and human... ...d change. Some animals eat plants. Some ... ...r animals. Other animals and humans may ... ...oth plants and animals.

Write your ideas, answer questions, make notes, and record activity results right on these pages.

▶ Dr... a food you like ... at.

Learn science concepts and skills by interacting with every page.

Labs & Activities

Science is all about doing.

Exciting investigations for every lesson.

Ask questions and test your ideas.

Draw conclusions and share what you learn.

How Does the Sun Warm Our Homes?

How does solar energy warm our homes? Make a model to find out.

Materials

cardboard box   tape

scissors   2 thermometers

plastic wrap

1. Use the box and the plastic wrap to make a model house. Caution! Be careful when using scissors.

2. Tape one thermometer into a window of the house. Record the temperatures on both thermometers.

3. Put the house in a sunny spot. Lay the other thermometer next to the house. Wait 1 hour. Record both temperatures again. Compare the numbers.

e-Learning & Virtual Labs

Digital lessons and virtual labs provide e-learning options for every lesson of *Science Fusion*.

sciencefusion

Unit 3 Lesson 1 : H

The water cycle

precipitation

The water dries up, and soon the puddle is gone.
But this water didn't disappear — it entered another part of the water cycle.

anges Your Heart Rate?

Look at the heart rate bar graph. Move your cursor over it to read the heart rate. Wait until the heart rate stays the same.

Standing

Walking

Running

Heart rate

172
152
132
112
92
72

Per min.

Observations		—
Activity level	Heartbeat rate	
Standing		
Walking		
Running		

Look at the heart rate bar graph. Move your cursor over it to read the heart rate. Wait until the heart rate stays the same.

On your own or with a group, explore science concepts in a digital world.

360° of Inquiry

Contents

Levels of Inquiry Key ■ DIRECTED ■ GUIDED ■ INDEPENDENT

THE NATURE OF SCIENCE AND S.T.E.M.

Unit 1—Work Like a Scientist 1

Lesson 1 How Do We Use Inquiry Skills? 3
Inquiry Flipchart p. 2—Hand in Hand/Do You See What I See?

Lesson 2 How Do We Use Science Tools? 13
Inquiry Flipchart p. 3—Hold It!/Objects Up Close

People in Science: Anders Celsius 21

Inquiry Lesson 3 What Tools Can We Use? 23
Inquiry Flipchart p. 4—What Tools Can We Use?

Lesson 4 How Do Scientists Think? 25
Inquiry Flipchart p. 5—Everything in Balance/Rule It!

Inquiry Lesson 5 How Do We Solve a Problem? 35
Inquiry Flipchart p. 6—How Do We Solve a Problem?

Unit 1 Review 37

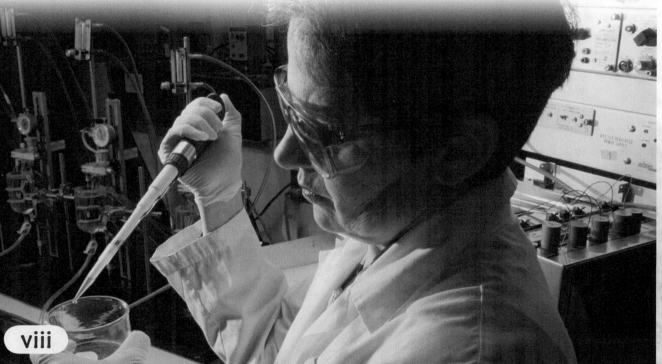

✓ Unit 2—Technology and Our World......... 41

Lesson 1 What Is the Design Process? 43
Inquiry Flipchart p. 7—Balloon Car/Parachute Puzzle

Inquiry Lesson 2 How Can We Use the Design Process? 55
Inquiry Flipchart p. 8—How Can We Use the Design Process?

Lesson 3 What Is Technology? 57
Inquiry Flipchart p. 9—Don't Break It!/Grab It!

Inquiry Lesson 4 How Can We Improve Technology? 69
Inquiry Flipchart p. 10—How Can We Improve Technology?

Careers in Science: Roller Coaster Designer 71

Unit 2 Review 73

LIFE SCIENCE

Unit 3—All About Animals 77

Lesson 1 What Are Animal Needs? 79
`Inquiry Flipchart` p. 11—Raising Crickets/An Animal I Know

S.T.E.M. Engineering and Technology: On the Farm 89
`Inquiry Flipchart` p. 12—Design It: Guard the Lettuce!

Lesson 2 What Are Some Kinds of Animals? 91
`Inquiry Flipchart` p. 13—Feathers and Hair/Compare Animals

Inquiry Lesson 3 How Do Body Coverings Help Animals? 103
`Inquiry Flipchart` p. 14—How Do Body Coverings Help Animals?

Lesson 4 What Are Some Animal Life Cycles? 105
`Inquiry Flipchart` p. 15—Where's the Caterpillar?/What's My Life Cycle?

People in Science: Salim Ali 117

Lesson 5 What Are Fossils? 119
`Inquiry Flipchart` p. 16—Fossil Dig/Model Fossils

Inquiry Lesson 6 How Can We Model a Fossil? 129
`Inquiry Flipchart` p. 17—How Can We Model a Fossil?

Unit 3 Review 131

Unit 4—All About Plants 135

Lesson 1 What Are Plant Needs? 137
Inquiry Flipchart p. 18—Block the Light/Airtight Seal

S.T.E.M. Engineering and Technology: Bringing Water to Plants 145
Inquiry Flipchart p. 19—Compare It: Drip Tips

Inquiry Lesson 2 What Do Plants Need to Grow? 147
Inquiry Flipchart p. 20—What Do Plants Need to Grow?

Lesson 3 What Are Some Plant Parts? 149
Inquiry Flipchart p. 21—Plant Stems/Plant Parts

Lesson 4 What Are Some Plant Life Cycles? 159
Inquiry Flipchart p. 22—Bud a Spud!/Speedy Seed Race

Inquiry Lesson 5 How Does a Bean Plant Grow? 171
Inquiry Flipchart p. 23—How Does a Bean Plant Grow?

People in Science: Dr. Maria Elena Zavala 173

Unit 4 Review 175

Unit 5—Environments for Living Things.. 179

Lesson 1 How Do Plants and Animals Need One Another? 181
Inquiry Flipchart p. 24—Helpful Plants/Model a Food Chain

Lesson 2 How Are Living Things Adapted to Their Environments? . 193
Inquiry Flipchart p. 25—Design a Bird/Waxy Leaves

Inquiry Lesson 3 Can Plants Survive in Different Environments?... 205
Inquiry Flipchart p. 26—Can Plants Survive in Different Environments?

**S.T.E.M. Engineering and Technology: Technology
and the Environment** 207
Inquiry Flipchart p. 27—Design It: Water Filter

Lesson 4 How Do Environments Change Over Time? 209
Inquiry Flipchart p. 28—Flood!/Plan to Help

Careers in Science: Environmental Scientist. 219

Unit 5 Review 221

EARTH SCIENCE

Unit 6—Earth and Its Resources. 225

Lesson 1 What Changes Earth? 227
Inquiry Flipchart p. 29—Earth Shake/Erosion Made Easy

Careers in Science: Geologist. 239

Lesson 2 What Are Natural Resources? 241
Inquiry Flipchart p. 30—Looking at Lunch/Product Hunt

S.T.E.M. Engineering and Technology: How It's Made: Cotton Shirt . . . 253
Inquiry Flipchart p. 31—Test It: Strong Buildings

Inquiry Lesson 3 How Can We Classify Plant Products? 255
Inquiry Flipchart p. 32—How Can We Classify Plant Products?

Unit 6 Review 259

Unit 7—All About Weather 263

Lesson 1 How Does Weather Change? 265
Inquiry Flipchart p. 33—Weather Journal/Wind Watching

Inquiry Lesson 2 How Does the Sun Heat Earth? 275
Inquiry Flipchart p. 34—How Does the Sun Heat Earth?

Lesson 3 What Are Some Weather Patterns? 277
Inquiry Flipchart p. 35—Take My Temperature/Highs and Lows

Inquiry Lesson 4 How Can We Measure Precipitation? 287
Inquiry Flipchart p. 36—How Can We Measure Precipitation?

Lesson 5 How Do Seasons Affect Living Things? 289
Inquiry Flipchart p. 37—Can You See Me?/Seasons Survey

S.T.E.M. Engineering and Technology: Watching Weather 299
Inquiry Flipchart p. 38—Improvise It: Weather Station

Lesson 6 How Can We Prepare for Severe Weather? 301
Inquiry Flipchart p. 39—Make Your Own Tornado/Keep It Safe!

Careers in Science: Storm Chaser 309

Unit 7 Review 311

Unit 8—The Solar System 315

Lesson 1 What Are Planets and Stars? 317
Inquiry Flipchart p. 40—Seeing Stars/Go Into Orbit

People in Science: Annie Jump Cannon 327

Lesson 2 What Causes Day and Night? 329
Inquiry Flipchart p. 41—Telling Time/Shadow Changes

S.T.E.M. Engineering and Technology: Eye on the Sky 339
Inquiry Flipchart p. 42—Improvise It: Telescope

Inquiry Lesson 3 How Can We Model Day and Night? 341
Inquiry Flipchart p. 43—How Can We Model Day and Night?

Unit 8 Review 343

PHYSICAL SCIENCE

Unit 9—Changes in Matter 347

Lesson 1 What Is Matter? 349
Inquiry Flipchart p. 44—Mass in the Balance/Property Scavenger Hunt

Inquiry Lesson 2 How Can We Compare Volumes? 361
Inquiry Flipchart p. 45—How Can We Compare Volumes?

S.T.E.M. Engineering and Technology: Kitchen Technology 363
Inquiry Flipchart p. 46—Think About Process: Write a Recipe

Lesson 3 How Does Matter Change? 365
Inquiry Flipchart p. 47—Evaporate Rate/What Melts?

Inquiry Lesson 4 How Can Water Change States? 373
Inquiry Flipchart p. 48—How Can Water Change States?

People in Science: Dr. Mei-Yin Chou 375

Unit 9 Review 377

Houghton Mifflin Harcourt Publishing Company

Unit 10—Energy and Magnets 381

Lesson 1 What Is Energy? 383
Inquiry Flipchart p. 49—A Change of Light/Turn Up the Heat

People in Science: Dr. Lawnie Taylor 395

Lesson 2 What Are Magnets? 397
Inquiry Flipchart p. 50—Action at a Distance/Magnetic Attraction

S.T.E.M. Engineering and Technology: Magnets All Around 407
Inquiry Flipchart p. 51—Design It: Use Magnets

Inquiry Lesson 3 How Strong Is a Magnet? 409
Inquiry Flipchart p. 52—How Strong Is a Magnet?

Unit 10 Review 411

Interactive Glossary R1

Index R24

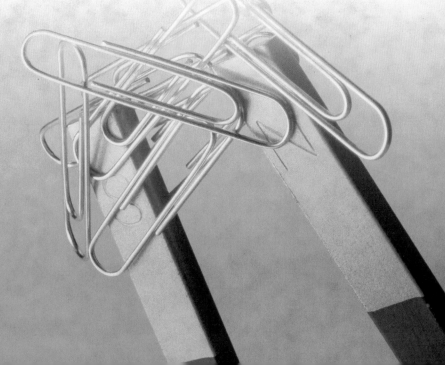

UNIT 1
Work Like a Scientist

Big Idea

Scientists ask questions about the world around them. They find answers by investigating through many methods.

Thomas Edison's lab

I Wonder Why
Scientists use tools to find out about things. Why?
Turn the page to find out.

Here's Why Tools help scientists learn more than they could with just their senses.

In this unit, you will explore this Big Idea, the Essential Questions, and the Investigations on the Inquiry Flipchart.

Levels of Inquiry Key ■ DIRECTED ■ GUIDED ■ INDEPENDENT

Big Idea Scientists ask questions about the world around them. They find answers by investigating through many methods.

Essential Questions

Lesson 1 How Do We Use Inquiry Skills? 3
Inquiry Flipchart p. 2—Hand in Hand/Do You See What I See?

Lesson 2 How Do We Use Science Tools? 13
Inquiry Flipchart p. 3—Hold It!/Objects Up Close

People in Science: Anders Celsius 21

Inquiry Lesson 3 What Tools Can We Use? 23
Inquiry Flipchart p. 4—What Tools Can We Use?

Lesson 4 How Do Scientists Think? 25
Inquiry Flipchart p. 5—Everything in Balance/Rule It!

Inquiry Lesson 5 How Do We Solve a Problem? 35
Inquiry Flipchart p. 6—How Do We Solve a Problem?

Unit 1 Review 37

Now I Get the Big Idea!

Science Notebook

Before you begin each lesson, be sure to write your thoughts about the Essential Question.

Essential Question

How Do We Use Inquiry Skills?

🧠 Engage Your Brain!

Find the answer in this lesson.

You tell how these flowers are alike and different.

You are
_____ them.

Active Reading

Lesson Vocabulary

1 Preview the lesson.

2 Write the vocabulary term here.

_____

Use Inquiry Skills

Inquiry skills help people find out information. Inquiry skills help people plan and do tests.

These children use inquiry skills to do a task for school. They are observing. Observe means to use your five senses to learn about things.

Active Reading

Find the sentence that tells the meaning of **observe**. Draw a line under the sentence.

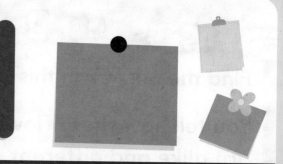

What can we observe in my backyard?

Danny and Sophie want to observe things in the backyard. They plan an investigation. They plan how to find out what they want to know. They also predict, or make a good guess, about what they will observe.

▶ **This page names three inquiry skills. Circle the name for one of the skills.**

Explore the Backyard

Danny and Sophie head out to the backyard to begin their task. Danny finds the length and the height of the birdhouse. He measures it with a ruler.

Active Reading

Find the sentence that explains what it means to **measure**. Draw a line under the sentence.

They use inquiry skills to learn more about the backyard.

Sophie compares leaves. She observes how they are alike and how they are different. She may also classify, or sort, many leaves in the backyard by the way they are alike.

▶ **Look at Sophie's leaves. Put them in order of size from smallest to largest.**

_____ _____ _____

Model and Infer

Now Danny and Sophie draw a map of the backyard. They are making a model to show what something is like. You could also make a model to show how something works.

My Backyard

birch tree

rose bush

maple tree

bird bath

bird house

Active Reading

Find the sentences that explain what it means to **make a model**. Draw a line under the sentences.

8

Danny and Sophie use one more inquiry skill. They infer. They use what they know to answer a question—Are there any living things in the backyard? They can infer that the backyard is home to many plants and animals.

▶ Think about what you know about winter. Infer what Danny and Sophie might observe in the backyard during winter.

_____

_____

Sum It Up!

① Complete It!

Fill in the blank.

How are measuring, observing, and predicting alike?

They are all

_____ .

② Circle It!

Circle the skill name to match the meaning.

Which one means to choose steps you will do to learn something?

infer

plan an investigation

classify

③ Draw and Write It!

Observe something outside. Then draw and write to record your observations.

_____

_____

Brain Check

Name _____

Word Play

Read each clue below. Then unscramble the letters to write the correct answer.

| observe | compare | measure | infer |

1 to find the size or amount of something

s e m a r e u _____

2 to use your senses to learn about something

b o s r e e v _____

3 to observe how things are alike and different

p o c r a m e _____

4 to use what you know to answer a question

f n i r e _____

© Houghton Mifflin Harcourt Publishing Company

Apply Concepts

Match each inquiry skill to its meaning.

to make a good guess about what will happen	plan an investigation
to sort things by how they are alike	classify
to show what something is like or how it works	predict
to follow steps to answer a question	make a model

Take It Home!

Family Members: Work with your child to measure two objects in your home. Have your child compare the two objects and tell which is larger.

Essential Question

How Do We Use Science Tools?

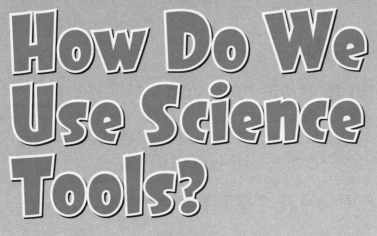

Engage Your Brain!

Find the answer to the question in the lesson.

What does a thermometer measure?

_____

Active Reading

Lesson Vocabulary

1 Preview the lesson.

2 Write the 2 vocabulary terms here.

_____   _____

Top Tools

You use tools every day. Tools are things that help you do a job. **Science tools** help you find out information.

A hand lens is one science tool. It helps you observe more details than with your eyes alone.

▶ What can you see through this hand lens? Circle it.

A hand lens makes things look larger.

Measuring Tools

You use some tools for measuring things. You use a **thermometer** to measure temperature. You use a measuring cup to measure amounts of liquids.

A thermometer measures temperature in units called degrees.

A measuring cup measures liquids in units called milliliters, cups, and ounces.

Measure More!

You use a tool called a scale to measure weight. You can use a balance to measure mass.

This scale measures weight in units called pounds and ounces.

▶ Name two things you can weigh on a scale.

_____

_____

This balance measures mass in units called grams and kilograms.

You use a ruler and a tape measure to measure distance as well as length, width, and height. Both tools measure in units called inches or centimeters.

▶ Circle the object the ruler is measuring.

A ruler measures objects with straight lines.

A tape measure can measure around an object.

17

Sum It Up!

① Answer It!

Write the answer to this question.

You want to measure how much water fits into a pail. What tool could you use?

_____

② Draw It!

Draw yourself using a measuring tool.

③ Mark It!

Mark an X on the tool that does _not_ measure.

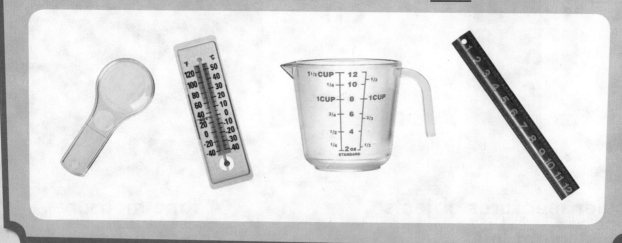

Brain Check

Name _____

Word Play

Match the name of each tool to its picture.

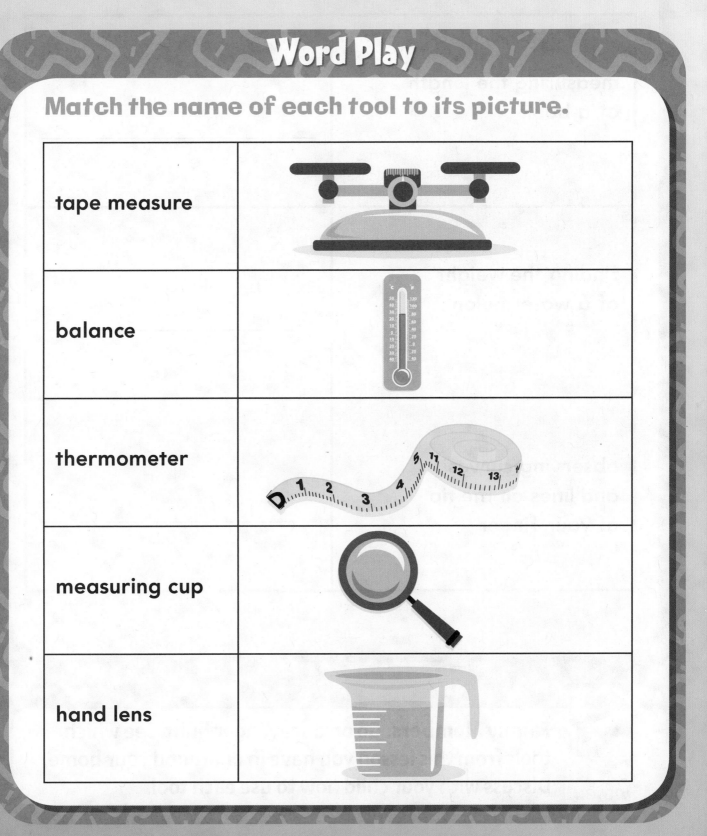

tape measure	
balance	
thermometer	
measuring cup	
hand lens	

Apply Concepts

Name the tool you could use for each job.

measuring the length of a book	_____
finding the weight of a watermelon	_____
observing curves and lines on the tip of your finger	_____

Family Members: Go on a scavenger hunt. See which tools from this lesson you have in or around your home. Discuss with your child how to use each tool.

1

In 1742, Celsius invented the Celsius scale to measure temperature.

2

The temperature at which water freezes on the Celsius scale is 0°.

4

Things to Know About
Anders Celsius

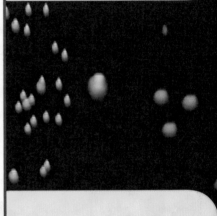

3

The temperature at which water boils on the Celsius scale is 100°.

4

Celsius was an astronomer, or a person who studies the stars and other things in space.

Celsius Match Up

1

▶ **Read each thermometer. Write the number that matches the correct temperature in each picture.**

2

3

▶ **How does a temperature scale help you tell about the weather?**

_____

_____

Name _____

Essential Question

What Tools Can We Use?

Set a Purpose

Write what you want to find out.

_____

_____

Think About the Procedure

1 Which science tool did you choose? What does it do?

_____

_____

2 How will the tool help you observe the object?

_____

_____

Record Your Data

Record your observations in this chart.

My Object _____	
My Tool _____	
What I Learned Without the Tool	What I Learned With the Tool

Draw Conclusions

How can a science tool help you learn more about an object?

_____

_____

_____

Ask More Questions

What other questions can you ask about how science tools are used?

_____

_____

_____

Essential Question

How Do Scientists Think?

Engage Your Brain!

Find the answer in the lesson.

When scientists

_____

they follow steps and use tools to answer a question.

Active Reading

Lesson Vocabulary

1. Preview the lesson.

2. Write the 4 vocabulary terms here.

_____ _____

_____ _____

Let's Observe It!

Scientists **investigate**. They plan and do a test to answer a question or solve a problem. They use inquiry skills and science tools to help them.

There are many ways to investigate. But many scientists follow a sequence, or order of events. Here's one possible sequence. First, scientists may observe and ask a question.

Active Reading

Clue words can help you find the order of things. **First** is a clue word. Circle this clue word in the paragraph above.

Does food coloring spread faster in cold water or warm water?

cold

Now, scientists can make a hypothesis. A **hypothesis** is a statement that can be tested. Then scientists plan a fair test. The scientists list the materials they will need and the steps they will take to do their test.

Food coloring spreads faster in warm water.

food coloring

warm

27

Let's Test It!

Next, the scientists are ready to do their test. They follow their plan and record what they observe.

Active Reading

Clue words can help you find the order of things. **Next** is a clue word. Circle this clue word in the paragraph above.

These children test whether food coloring spreads faster in cold water or warm water.

After the test, scientists **draw conclusions**. They use the information they have gathered to decide if their results support the hypothesis. Finally, they write or draw to **communicate** what they learned.

warm

▶ How does the temperature of water affect how fast the food coloring spreads? Draw a conclusion.

_____

_____

_____

▶ What else could a scientist test with water and food coloring?

_____

_____

_____

Let's Check Again!

Scientists do the same test a few times.
They need to make sure that they get similar results
every time. In this investigation, the food coloring
should spread faster in warm water every time.

Our Food Colori

Monday

Wednesday

▶ Look at the **warm** cup for both Monday and Friday. Draw a conclusion. Color in the **warm** cup for Wednesday to show what it should look like.

Test

cold   warm

Friday

Do the Math!
Measure Length

Choose an object. Use a ruler to measure the object's length. Measure it three times. Record.

Length of _____	
Measure 1	
Measure 2	
Measure 3	

1. How do your numbers compare?

_____

_____

2. Why do you think so?

_____

_____

_____

Sum It Up!

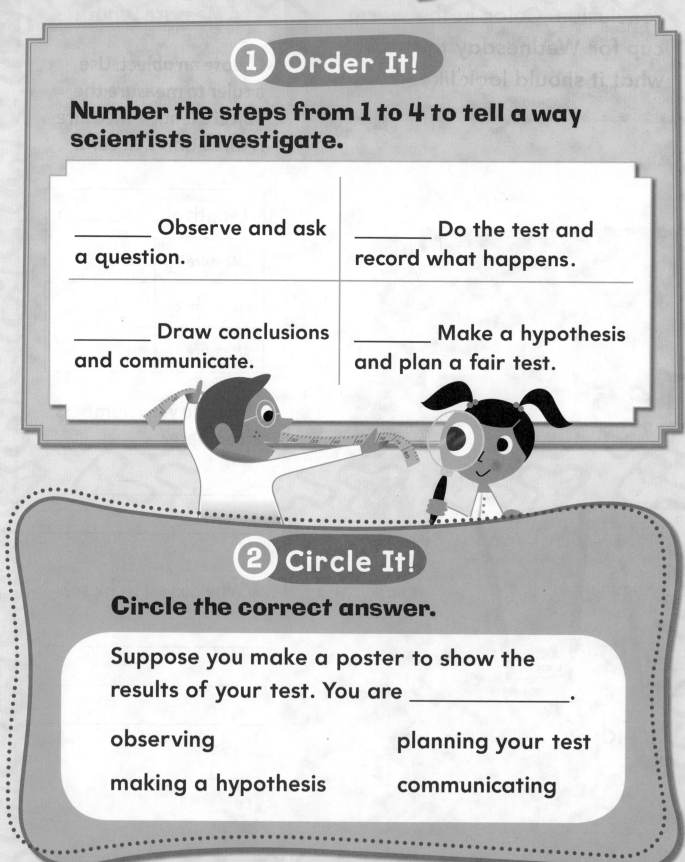

1 Order It!

Number the steps from 1 to 4 to tell a way scientists investigate.

_____ Observe and ask a question.

_____ Do the test and record what happens.

_____ Draw conclusions and communicate.

_____ Make a hypothesis and plan a fair test.

2 Circle It!

Circle the correct answer.

Suppose you make a poster to show the results of your test. You are _____.

observing   planning your test

making a hypothesis   communicating

Name _____

Word Play

Circle the word to complete each sentence.

① You use inquiry skills and science tools to learn. You _____.

communicate   investigate

② You take the first step to do an investigation. You _____.

draw conclusions   observe

③ You make a statement that you can test. You make a _____.

hypothesis   conclusion

④ You use information you gathered to explain what you learned. You _____.

draw conclusions   observe

⑤ You write to tell about the results of a test. You _____.

communicate   ask a question

Apply Concepts

These steps show a test some children did. Label each box with a step from this lesson.

The children look at an ice cube. They ask—Will it melt in the sun?

Observe and _____.

They form a statement that the ice cube will melt in the sun.

_____.

They follow their plan. The ice cube melts! They decide that the sun's heat caused the ice to melt.

Test and _____.

The children write and draw to tell the results of their test.

_____.

Family Members: Work with your child to plan an investigation. Use the steps from this lesson.

Take It Home!

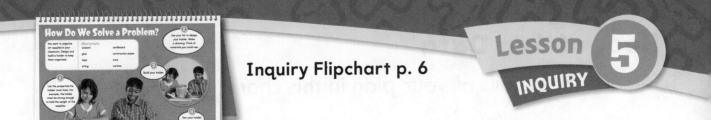
Name _____

Essential Question

How Do We Solve a Problem?

Set a Purpose

What problem do you want to solve?

_____

_____

Think About the Procedure

1 Why do you make a list of the properties the holder must have?

_____

_____

2 Why do you design your holder before you build it?

_____

_____

Record Your Data

Record the details of your plan in this chart.

The Problem	
My Plan	
Materials I need	

Draw Conclusions

Sometimes it is helpful to make a model first before making the real thing. How can making a model help you solve a problem?

_____

_____

Ask More Questions

What other questions do you have about designing and making models to solve problems?

_____

_____

Unit 1 Review

Vocabulary Review

Use the terms in the box to complete the sentences.

> communicate
> investigate
> thermometer

1. When you draw or write, you
   _____.

2. A tool that measures temperature is a(n)
   _____.

3. When you plan and do a test to answer a
   question, you _____.

Science Concepts

Fill in the letter of the choice that best answers the question.

4. Sumeet looks at the sky before he goes to school. It is dark and cloudy outside. What skill is Sumeet using?

   Ⓐ comparing
   Ⓑ inferring
   Ⓒ observing

5. Victor weighs a melon on a scale. The melon weighs 3 pounds. Ana also measures the weight of the same melon. What should Ana observe?

   Ⓐ The melon weighs 2 pounds.
   Ⓑ The melon weighs 3 pounds.
   Ⓒ The melon weighs 4 pounds.

6. Reem uses this tool to find the length of a book.

| 1 2 3 4 5 6 7 8 9 10 11 12 |
| centimeters |

What is she doing?

Ⓐ classifying

Ⓑ inferring

Ⓒ measuring

7. Jia wants to find out how the temperature in the afternoon compares to the morning temperature. What should she do?

Ⓐ Infer the afternoon temperature. Then compare it to the morning temperature.

Ⓑ Measure the afternoon temperature. Then compare it to the morning temperature.

Ⓒ Predict the afternoon temperature. Then compare it to the morning temperature.

8. Lea investigates the answer to a question. Then she repeats her experiment. Which will **most likely** be true?

Ⓐ The results will be the same.

Ⓑ The results will be different.

Ⓒ She cannot compare the results.

9. Carlos finishes an investigation. He draws this picture in a notebook.

Why does Carlos draw the picture?

Ⓐ to plan the investigation

Ⓑ to predict what will happen

Ⓒ to record what he observed

10. Jared knows that his two blocks are the same color but different shapes. How does he know?

Ⓐ He measures them.

Ⓑ He makes a model.

Ⓒ He observes and compares them.

11. You think that an ant and a butterfly have the same parts. Why would models help you find out if this is true?

Ⓐ The models would be the same size as the real insects.

Ⓑ The models would show parts that the real insects have.

Ⓒ Making models would mean that you do not have to make observations.

12. Kate wants to know whether a tree or a bush is taller. Which tool should she use?

Ⓐ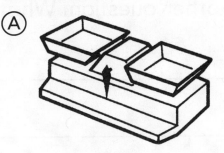

Ⓑ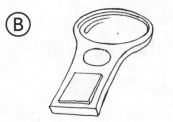

Ⓒ

Inquiry and the Big Idea
Write the answers to these questions.

13. You complete an investigation about plants. Now you have another question. What should you do?

_____

_____

14. Look at the picture.

a. What science tool is the boy using?

_____

b. What is he doing?

_____

UNIT 2
Technology and Our World

The Pyramids,
Indianapolis, Indiana

Big Idea

Engineers use a process to design new technology to meet human needs. Technology affects our everyday life and can affect the environment around us.

I Wonder How

An engineer planned a design for these buildings. How?
Turn the page to find out.

Here's How An engineer drew a plan for the buildings. The plan showed these interesting shapes.

In this unit, you will explore this Big Idea, the Essential Questions, and the Investigations on the Inquiry Flipchart.

Levels of Inquiry Key ■ DIRECTED ■ GUIDED ■ INDEPENDENT

Big Idea Engineers use a process to design new technology to meet human needs. Technology affects our everyday life and can affect the environment around us.

Essential Questions

Lesson 1 What Is the Design Process?. 43
Inquiry Flipchart p. 7—Balloon Car/Parachute Puzzle

Inquiry Lesson 2 How Can We Use the
Design Process? 55
Inquiry Flipchart p. 8—How Can We Use the Design Process?

Lesson 3 What Is Technology? 57
Inquiry Flipchart p. 9—Don't Break It!/Grab It!

Inquiry Lesson 4 How Can We Improve Technology?. 69
Inquiry Flipchart p. 10—How Can We Improve Technology?

🔬 Careers in Science: Roller Coaster Designer 71

Unit 2 Review 73

Now I Get the Big Idea!

Science Notebook

Before you begin each lesson, be sure to write your thoughts about the Essential Question.

Essential Question

What Is the Design Process?

Engage Your Brain!

Find the answer to the question in the lesson.

How could you keep the dog leashes from getting tangled?

You could _____

_____.

Active Reading

Lesson Vocabulary

1 Preview the lesson.

2 Write the 2 vocabulary terms here.

_____ _____

Get Real!

Look at the engineers at work! **Engineers** solve problems by using math and science. The answers they find help people.

Engineers work in many areas. Some engineers design cars. Some make robots. Others find ways to make the world cleaner or safer.

Active Reading

Find the sentence that tells the meaning of **engineers**. Draw a line under that sentence.

A civil engineer plans bridges and roads.

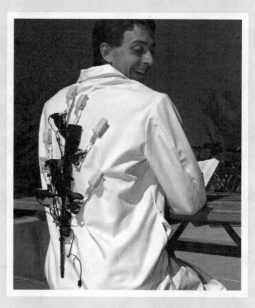

A robotics engineer designs robots.

The Design Process

How do engineers solve a problem? They use a design process. A **design process** is a set of steps that engineers follow to solve problems.

This engineer checks on a building project.

Circle the names of three kinds of engineers.

An aerospace engineer may work on airplanes or rockets.

A Tangled Mess!

When Kate walks her dogs, their leashes always get tangled. She needs to solve this problem. How can a design process help?

1 Find a Problem

Kate's first step is to name her problem. What is wrong? What does she want to do? Then Kate brainstorms ways to solve her problem.

Kate gets out her science notebook. She will keep good records. She will show how she plans and builds the solution to her problem.

Problem—
My dogs' leashes keep tangling.

Brainstorm solutions—

▶ Draw a way that Kate could solve her problem.

2 Plan and Build

Next, Kate chooses a solution to try. She makes a plan. She draws and labels her plan.

Kate chooses materials that are good for leashes. Look at Kate's materials. What materials would you choose?

Active Reading

Clue words can help you find the order of things. **Next** is a clue word. Draw a box around this clue word.

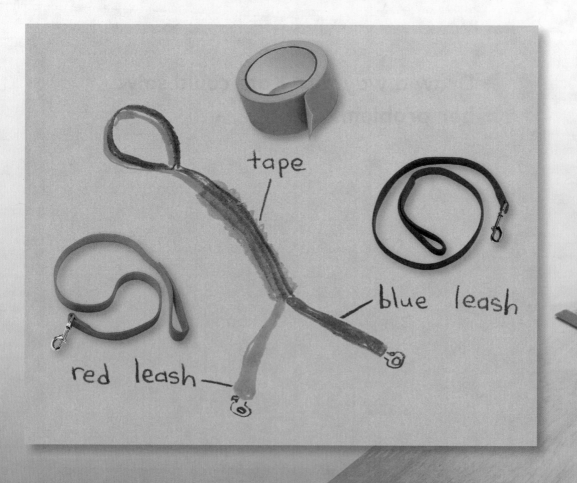

tape

red leash

blue leash

Kate follows her plan to make her new leash.
The new leash may be the solution to her problem!

► How does planning
help Kate build her
new leash?

_____

_____

③ Test and Improve

It is time for Kate to find out whether the new leash works. She tests it when she walks the dogs. Kate will know the leash works if it does not tangle.

4 Redesign

Kate thinks of ways to improve her new leash. She writes notes about how to make her design better.

5 Communicate

Kate shows the results of her test. She takes a picture of her design. She also writes about what happened during the test.

Ways to make the design better—make the leash parts or the handle longer.

My Results—
1. Red and blue parts of the new leash did not tangle.
2. My feet bumped the dogs as I walked.

▶ Circle the part of the results that tells about a problem with the leash.

Sum It Up!

1 Circle It!

Circle the step of the design process shown here.

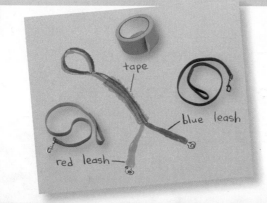

Test and Improve

Plan and Build

Find a Problem

2 Write It!

Write the answer to the question.

Why is it important to keep good records?

_____

_____

_____

_____

52

Name _____

Word Play

Write a term for each definition.

design process   materials   solution   test

steps that engineers follow to solve a problem

__ __ __ __ __ __   __ __ __ __ __ __ __ __
   1   3 2

the answer to a problem

__ __ __ __ __ __ __ __
        4   5

how you find out whether a solution works

__ __ __ __
  6

things you use to make a design

__ __ __ __ __ __ __ __ __
    7 8

Solve the riddle. Write the numbered
letters in order on the lines below.

I am a scientist who uses math and science
to solve problems. Who am I?

__ __ __ __ __ __ __ __
1 2 3 4 5 6 7 8

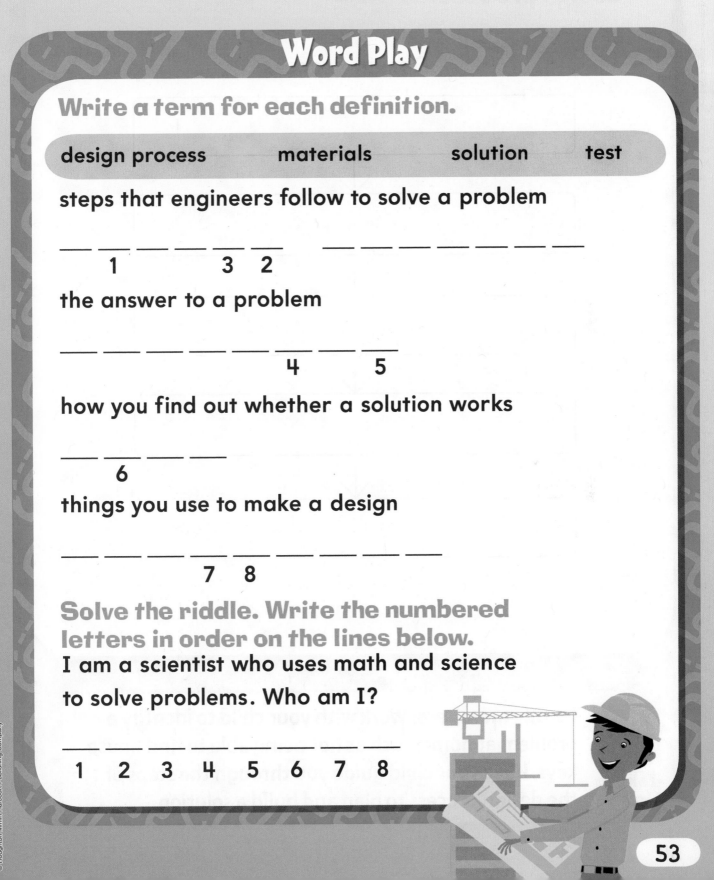

Apply Concepts

Complete the flowchart with the steps of the design process.

Design Process

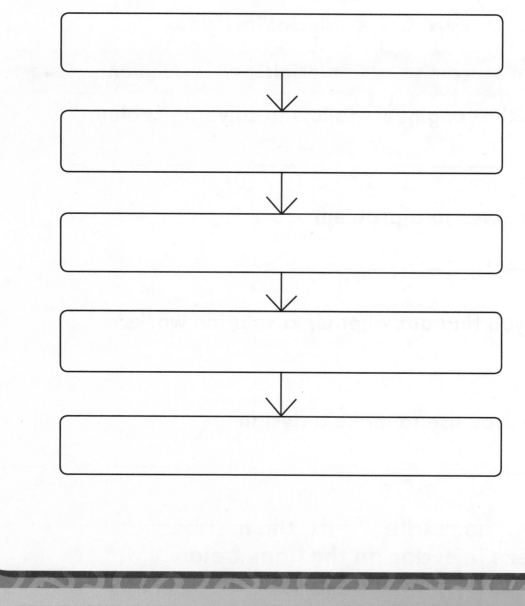

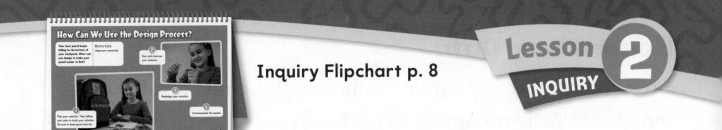

Name _____

Essential Question

How Can We Use the Design Process?

Set a Purpose

Tell what you want to do.

_____

_____

Think About the Procedure

1 Why do you need to plan your solution?

_____

_____

_____

2 Why do you need to test your solution?

_____

_____

_____

Record Your Data

Draw to communicate your solution and the test results. Label the materials. Write a caption to tell how your solution works.

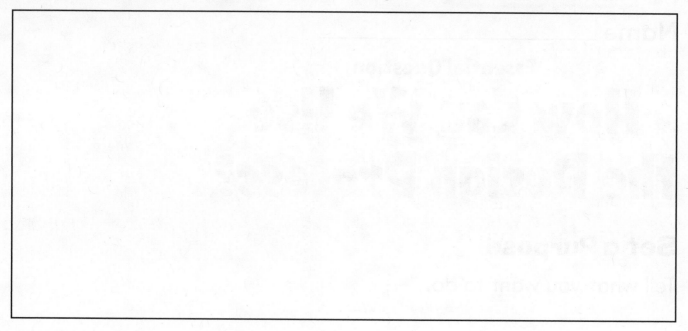

_____

Draw Conclusions

How did the design process help you solve the problem?

_____

_____

Ask More Questions

What other questions could you ask about using the design process?

_____

_____

Essential Question

What Is Technology?

Find the answer to the question in the lesson.

You use the technology in this picture every day.
What is it?

It is a

_____ .

Active Reading

Lesson Vocabulary

1 Preview the lesson.

2 Write the 2 vocabulary terms here.

_____   _____

By Design

Did you use a toothbrush or turn on a light today? Both a toothbrush and a light are kinds of technology. **Technology** is what engineers make to meet needs and solve problems. Anything people design to help us do things is technology.

Active Reading

Find the sentence that tells the meaning of **technology**. Draw a line under the sentence.

The bristles are curved to fit around teeth.

The grip makes it easy to hold the brush.

The pump pulls soap through the nozzle.

nozzle

▶ Name two kinds of **technology** you find around your bathroom sink.

_____

_____

_____

Everyday Technology

Technology is all around us. We use it every day. We depend on it at home and at school. Technology helps us do things. It helps us meet our needs. How have you used technology today?

Technology lights our homes. Electricity can produce light.

Do the Math!
Solve a Problem

Read the word problem. Answer the question.

The average person uses 80 gallons of water at home each day. How much water does a person use in 2 days? Show your work.

_____ gallons

When the power goes out, so do electric lights. What other technology could you use to light your home?

_____

_____

Technology helps bring clean water to our homes.

Technology helps us make food. An oven, stovetop, and microwave oven cook food and heat water.

Play It Safe

Technology can be helpful when we use it with care. It can be unsafe if we do not use it with care.

We should use each kind of technology the way it was designed to be used. We should wear safety gear if we need to. Using technology correctly helps us stay safe.

Active Reading

The main idea is the most important idea about something. Draw two lines under the main idea.

The things that keep us safe are technology, too!

The hard plastic keeps things out of the eyes.

Foam and the hard covering protect the head.

Straps hold the helmet in place.

▶ What technology keeps you safe in a car?

_____

_____

_____

Environmental Effects

Technology can affect the environment. An **environment** is all the living and nonliving things in a place.

Batteries, for example, are a helpful technology. They provide power to phones, cars, toys, and other things. But they can harm the environment, too.

When old batteries break down, they can pollute water and soil.

Some batteries can be used over and over again. Most batteries can be recycled. How do you think this helps the environment?

▶ Write two ways you can keep batteries from being thrown away.

_____

_____

_____

Sum It Up!

① Circle It!

Circle the examples of technology.

② Write It!

Write a way people depend on technology.

_____

_____

_____

③ Draw It

Draw a way you use technology to be safe.

Name _____

Word Play

Match each word to its meaning.

what engineers make to meet needs and solve problems	environment
all the living and nonliving things in a place	technology

Write two ways technology can affect the environment.

_____

_____

_____

_____

Apply Concepts

Fill in the chart. Write different kinds of technology.

Technology

Technology I Use Every Day
_____
_____

Technology I Must Use With Care
_____
_____

Technology That Affects the Environment
_____
_____

Take It Home!

Family Members: Ask your child to point out examples of technology in your home. Discuss how to use the technology safely.

Name _____

Essential Question

How Can We Improve Technology?

Set a Purpose

Tell what you want to find out.

_____

_____

Think About the Procedure

❶ What are some objects you could choose?

_____

_____

❷ How could you improve your object?

_____

Record Your Data

Draw to communicate your solution. Label your picture.

Draw Conclusions

How did your solution improve the object you chose?

_____

_____

_____

Ask More Questions

What other questions could you ask about improving technology?

_____

_____

_____

70

Ask a Roller Coaster Designer

What do roller coaster designers do?
We design roller coasters for amusement parks. We think up ideas for new rides. We also figure out how much they will cost to build.

Do designers work alone?
We work as a team with engineers to make a design. The design has to work and be safe and fun for riders. A factory then builds the ride.

How long does it take to build a roller coaster?
It usually takes about a year from design to finish. A simpler design takes less time.

Now It's Your Turn!

▶ What question would you ask a roller coaster designer?

_____

_____

_____

_____

Design Your Own Roller Coaster

▶ Draw your own roller coaster in the space below.

▶ Explain your design. Write about how your roller coaster moves.

_____

_____

_____

Unit 2 Review

Vocabulary Review

Use the terms in the box to complete the sentences.

> design process
> environment
> technology

1. A set of steps engineers follow to solve problems is a(n) _____.

2. What engineers make to meet needs and solve problems is _____.

3. All of the living and nonliving things in a place is a(n) _____.

Science Concepts

Fill in the letter of the choice that best answers the question.

4. What kind of work do engineers do?
   - (A) make new designs for people to buy
   - (B) invent new steps in the design process
   - (C) solve problems using math and science

5. How can technology affect an environment?
   - (A) It can help.
   - (B) It can hurt.
   - (C) It can help or hurt.

6. You chose these items to design a solution to a problem.

What step of the design process did you do?

Ⓐ Find a problem.

Ⓑ Plan and build.

Ⓒ Test and improve.

7. Which classroom object is an example of technology?

Ⓐ a pencil

Ⓑ a plant

Ⓒ a student

8. Why do engineers use the design process?

Ⓐ It is easy.

Ⓑ It helps them use tools.

Ⓒ It helps them solve problems.

9. Look at this object.

What is it an example of?

Ⓐ the design process

Ⓑ an engineer

Ⓒ technology

10. When do people use technology?

Ⓐ only when there is a problem

Ⓑ almost every day to meet their needs

Ⓒ only when they want to help the environment

11. You are following the steps in the design process. How can you tell whether a solution works?

Ⓐ Ask other people.

Ⓑ Draw and write about the solution.

Ⓒ Test the solution.

12. How is this person using technology?

Ⓐ to clean

Ⓑ to stay safe

Ⓒ to cook dinner

Inquiry and the Big Idea
Write the answers to these questions.

13. You need a way to carry six drink cans or bottles at the same time. Explain the steps you would follow to design a tool to solve your problem.

1. _____

2. _____

3. _____

4. _____

14. Look at the picture.

a. Identify how people use this technology.

_____

_____

b. What is good about this technology?

_____

c. What is bad about this technology?

_____

UNIT 3
All About Animals

Big Idea

There are many kinds of animals. They have certain needs.

sea turtle

I Wonder Why

Mother sea turtles bury their eggs in the sand. Why?

Turn the page to find out.

Here's Why Mother turtles need to keep their eggs warm and protected for the young turtles to hatch.

In this unit, you will explore this Big Idea, the Essential Questions, and the Investigations on the Inquiry Flipchart.

Levels of Inquiry Key ■ DIRECTED ■ GUIDED ■ INDEPENDENT

Track Your Progress

Big Idea There are many kinds of animals. They have certain needs.

Essential Questions

Lesson 1 **What Are Animal Needs?** 79
Inquiry Flipchart p. 11—Raising Crickets/An Animal I Know

S.T.E.M. **Engineering and Technology: On the Farm** 89
Inquiry Flipchart p. 12—Design It: Guard the Lettuce!

Lesson 2 **What Are Some Kinds of Animals?** 91
Inquiry Flipchart p. 13—Feathers and Hair/Compare Animals

Inquiry Lesson 3 **How Do Body Coverings Help Animals?** . .103
Inquiry Flipchart p. 14—How Do Body Coverings Help Animals?

Lesson 4 **What Are Some Animal Life Cycles?** 105
Inquiry Flipchart p. 15—Where's the Caterpillar?/What's My Life Cycle?

People in Science: Salim Ali 117

Lesson 5 **What Are Fossils?** 119
Inquiry Flipchart p. 16—Fossil Dig/Model Fossils

Inquiry Lesson 6 **How Can We Model a Fossil?** 129
Inquiry Flipchart p. 17—How Can We Model a Fossil?

Unit 3 Review 131

Now I Get the Big Idea!

Science Notebook

Before you begin each lesson, be sure to write your thoughts about the Essential Question.

Essential Question

What Are Animal Needs?

Engage Your Brain!

Find the answer to the question in the lesson.

How is a frog like a human?

Both need food

to _____ .

Active Reading

Lesson Vocabulary

1. Preview the lesson.

2. Write the 4 vocabulary terms here.

_____   _____

_____   _____

Just the Basics

Animals are living things. Humans are living things, too. Just like plants, animals and humans have basic needs. They must meet their basic needs in order to **survive**, or stay alive.

What basic need are these animals getting? How does this make animals like plants?

Active Reading

Circle the words that help you know what **survive** means.

Animals need water to survive.

Water Everywhere

Humans need water, too. Drinking water helps us survive. Water is also in other things we drink, such as milk and juice.

The water in this drink helps the girl get what she needs.

▶ Draw and label a picture to show what you like to drink.

It's in the Air!

Living things need oxygen to survive. Humans and many animals use body parts called **lungs** to get oxygen from the air. Humans and these animals take in the air through their mouths and noses.

Put a hand on your chest and take a deep breath. Can you feel your lungs taking in air?

This boy is swimming underwater. He is using a snorkel.

▶ Why do people need a snorkel to swim underwater?

_____

_____

It's in the Water!

Some animals, such as fish, use gills to take in oxygen. **Gills** are parts of an animal that take in oxygen from the water. Can you find the gill on the side of the fish's head?

▶ Label the part of the fish that takes in oxygen.

_____

Interpret a Table

Animal Breathing Rates

Use the chart to answer the questions.

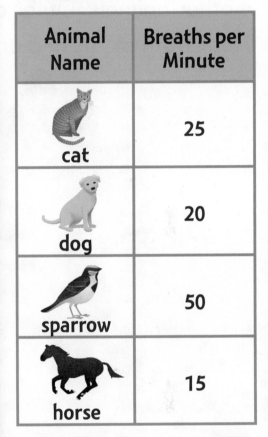

Animal Name	Breaths per Minute
cat	25
dog	20
sparrow	50
horse	15

1. How many more breaths per minute does a sparrow take than a cat?

_____

2. How many more breaths per minute does a dog take than a horse?

_____

Food for Thought

Food is an important need for animals and humans. Food helps animals and humans grow and change. Some animals eat plants. Some eat other animals. Other animals and humans may eat both plants and animals.

A giraffe eats the leaves from trees.

▶ Draw a food you like to eat.

Protection for All

Animals need space to move, find food, and grow. Humans and many animals also need shelter. A **shelter** is a safe place to live.

Humans also need something that animals do not need. We need clothes to protect our bodies from cold and rainy weather.

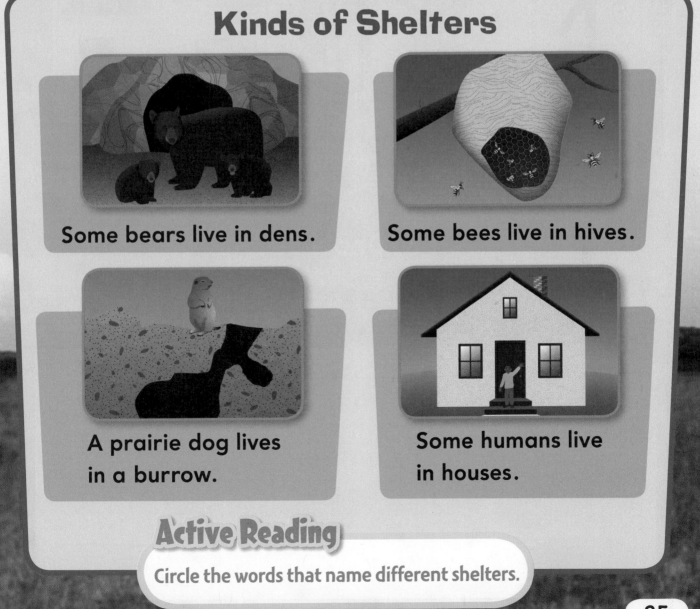

Kinds of Shelters

Some bears live in dens.

Some bees live in hives.

A prairie dog lives in a burrow.

Some humans live in houses.

Active Reading

Circle the words that name different shelters.

Sum It Up!

① Circle It!

Circle the living thing that does <u>not</u> use lungs to get oxygen.

② Mark It!

Cross out the thing that humans do <u>not</u> need to survive.

③ Draw It!

Draw an animal in its shelter.
Show the animal meeting another need.

Brain Check

Word Play

Name _____

Read the words and the clues.
Write the word that goes with each clue.

| lungs | gills | shelter | survive | oxygen |

1 I am a safe place to live. ___ ___ ___ ___ ___ ___ ___

2 We are the body parts that you use to take in oxygen.

___ ___ ___ ___ ___

3 I mean to stay alive. ___ ___ ___ ___ ___ ___ ___

4 We are the body parts that fish and tadpoles use to stay alive in water.

___ ___ ___ ___ ___

5 I am in the air you breathe. ___ ___ ___ ___ ___ ___

© Houghton Mifflin Harcourt Publishing Company

Apply Concepts

Complete the Venn diagram. Show how animal needs and plant needs are alike and different.

Animal Needs   Both   Plant Needs

Complete the sentence.
Tell about the main idea of this lesson.

Basic needs are the things that animals and plants

need to _____ .

Family Members: Talk about animals that you and your child have or know. Ask your child to tell how those animals meet their basic needs.

On the Farm

Farm System

A farm is a kind of system. A system is a group of parts that work together. All parts must work for the whole system to run well. Some parts of a farm are the crops, animals, people, and tools.

Farmers use tools, such as fences, to care for their crops and animals.

Farmers plan where to plant crops. They know what times of year are best to plant.

What to Do?

Read the story. Then write how you would solve the problem.

You have a small farm. Everything is working well. One day, wind knocks down part of a fence on your farm.

1. How could the broken fence affect the farm?
2. What would you do to fix the problem?
3. How do you think your solution will help?

1. _____

_____

2. _____

3. _____

Build On It!

Design solutions to other problems on a farm. Complete **Design It: Guard the Lettuce!** on the Inquiry Flipchart.

Essential Question

What Are Some Kinds of Animals?

Engage Your Brain!

Find the answer to the question in the lesson.

A penguin cannot fly. But it's still a bird. Why?

It _____ .

Active Reading

Lesson Vocabulary

1 Preview the lesson.

2 Write the 6 vocabulary terms here.

_____ _____

_____ _____

_____ _____

Animal Stars

Many kinds of animals live on Earth. Animals are many different shapes, colors, and sizes. Different animals have different body parts and coverings. Animals have their young in different ways, too. Here are some stars of the animal world!

Active Reading

The main idea is the most important idea about something. Draw two lines under the main idea.

Some animals lay eggs.

Other animals give birth to live young.

Animal Body Parts

Fins help fish swim and balance. They also help fish steer.

Suction cups help the frog climb and hold on.

An elephant can use its trunk to grab and lift. It can also use its trunk to drink water.

▶ Think of an animal. Draw how it uses its body parts to move.

By a Hair

A **mammal** has hair or fur that covers its skin. Most mammal mothers give birth to live young. The young drink milk from their mothers' bodies.

Active Reading

Find the sentence that tells the meaning of **mammal**. Draw a line under the sentence.

Mammals breathe air. Manatees rise to the top of water to breathe air.

Many mammals have legs to move. This antelope uses its legs to run fast.

A Fine Feather

A **bird** has feathers that cover its skin. Birds have wings, too. Feathers and wings help most birds fly. Birds use beaks to get food and build nests. Bird mothers lay eggs to have young.

Not all birds can fly. A kiwi has feathers and wings, but it cannot fly.

This pelican has wide wings. It uses its long, deep beak to scoop fish.

▶ Name the body covering for each group.

mammals	birds

Scale Up

A **reptile** has dry skin covered with scales. Most reptiles walk on four legs. Most reptile mothers lay eggs. Most reptile mothers lay their eggs on land.

Snakes are reptiles, but they do not have legs. Some snake mothers give birth to live young.

A tortoise has a hard shell. The shell helps keep it safe.

On Land and Water

An **amphibian** lives in water and on land. Most amphibians have smooth, wet skin. They lay their eggs in water. Young amphibians live in the water. Most adult amphibians live on land.

This toad is an amphibian, but it has rough, bumpy skin. Its strong back legs help it jump.

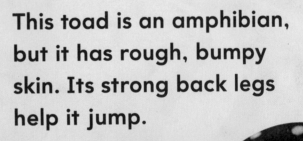

This newt is an amphibian. It has smooth, wet skin.

▶ Write where each group lays its eggs.

reptiles	amphibians

A Fish Story

Fish live in water and take in oxygen through gills. Fins help fish swim and balance. Most fish have scales. Most fish lay eggs.

moorish idols

betta

Moorish idols and bettas are fish. They lay eggs in water.

Sharks are fish. They give birth to live young.

As Snug as a Bug

An **insect** has three body parts and six legs. It also has a hard outer body covering, but no bones. Most insects live on land. Many insects can fly.

One part of an insect is its head. Where is the head on these insects?

ladybug

butterfly

grasshopper

▶ Write where each group lives.

fish	insects
_____	_____
_____	_____

Sum It Up!

① Mark It!

Mark an X on each amphibian. Circle each reptile.

② Label It!

Draw a fish. Label its parts.

③ Match It!

Match the parts to what they do.

fins	help most birds fly
gills	help fish take in oxygen
wings	help fish swim

Name _____

Word Play

Use the words below to label each animal.

fish   amphibian   insect   bird   reptile   mammal

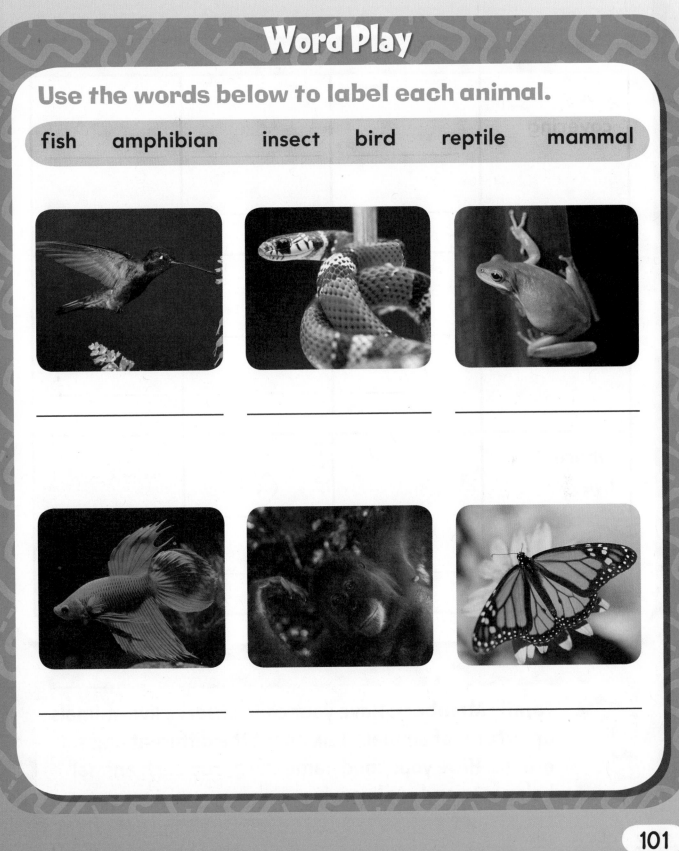

_____   _____   _____

_____   _____   _____

Apply Concepts

Fill in the chart. Show what you know about each animal.

Animals

	manatee	toad	kiwi
body covering	_____ _____	_____ _____	_____ _____
how it has its young	_____ _____	_____ _____	_____ _____
where it lives	_____ _____	_____ _____	_____ _____

© Houghton Mifflin Harcourt Publishing Company

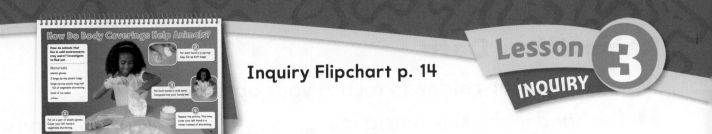
Name _____

Essential Question

How Do Body Coverings Help Animals?

Set a Purpose

Write what you want to find out during this investigation.

_____

_____

Think About the Procedure

1 What body covering is the shortening like?

_____

_____

2 What body covering is the mitten like?

_____

_____

Record Your Data

Write **warmer** or **colder** to record your observations.

1 The hand in the shortening felt _____ than the other hand.

2 The hand in the mitten felt _____ than the other hand.

Draw Conclusions

1 Does fat keep animals warm in cold environments? Tell how you know.

_____

_____

_____

2 Does fur keep animals warm? Tell how you know.

_____

_____

_____

Ask More Questions

What other questions can you ask about animal body coverings?

_____

_____

Essential Question

What Are Some Animal Life Cycles?

Engage Your Brain!

Find the answer to the riddle in this lesson.

When is a frog not like a frog?

When it is

a _____.

Active Reading

Lesson Vocabulary

1 Preview the lesson.

2 Write the 6 vocabulary terms here.

_____   _____

_____   _____

_____   _____

Animal Start-Ups

A dog can have puppies. A cat can have kittens. Adult animals can **reproduce**, or have young. Animals such as puppies and kittens look like their parents. How does a kitten look like an adult cat?

Other young animals look very different from their parents. They go through changes and become like their parents.

A young butterfly does not look like its parents.

A young cat looks like its parents.

▶ Name another animal that looks like its parents.

_____

What's in the Egg?

Many animals begin life by hatching from an egg. Animals change as they grow. The changes that happen to an animal during its life make up its **life cycle**.

▶ How are the animals in this chart alike?

_____

_____

Animal Life Cycles

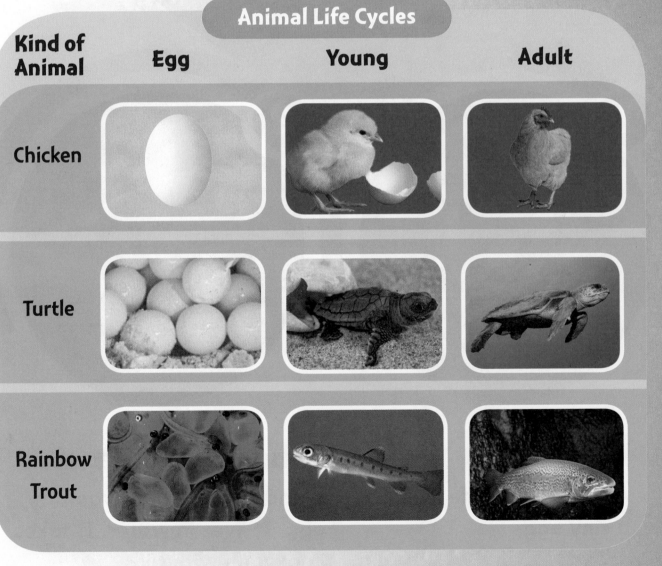

Kind of Animal	Egg	Young	Adult
Chicken			
Turtle			
Rainbow Trout			

Egg

A frog begins life inside a tiny egg.

Young Tadpole

A tadpole hatches from the egg. It lives in water. It takes in oxygen with gills.

Hatch, Swim, Hop

Did you know that a frog begins life inside a tiny egg? The young frog goes through changes to become an adult. These changes are called **metamorphosis**.

3

4

Growing Tadpole

The tadpole gets bigger. It grows four legs. Later, it loses its tail.

Frog

The adult can live on land or in the water. It hops. It breathes with lungs.

Polar Parenting

It is late October. A female polar bear gets a shelter ready for her cubs. She digs a den in the snow. The den will keep her young warm and safe. She gives birth in winter.

▶ How is a polar bear's life cycle different from a frog's life cycle?

_____

Newborn

A polar bear cub is born inside the den. It drinks milk from its mother's body.

Growing Cub

The cub begins to explore outside the den.

We'll stay with our mother for almost three years, until we're grown up.

3

4

Young Polar Bear

The young polar bear learns to swim and hunt.

Adult Polar Bear

The adult polar bear can live on its own. It can have its own young.

The Mighty Monarch

A monarch butterfly has a life cycle, too. An adult female butterfly lays a tiny egg. The egg is so small it is hard to see. This picture shows a close-up of an egg on a leaf.

1 egg

▶ Why do you think a butterfly egg is so small?

_____

_____

2 larva

A tiny **larva**, or caterpillar, hatches from the egg. A caterpillar is a young butterfly. The larva eats a lot and grows quickly.

Then the larva stops eating and moving. The larva becomes a pupa. It makes a hard covering.

A **pupa** goes through metamorphosis inside the covering. It grows wings. Many other changes also happen.

3 pupa

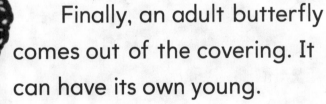

4 adult

Finally, an adult butterfly comes out of the covering. It can have its own young.

Active Reading

Clue words can help you find the order of events. Draw a box around the clue words **then** and **finally**.

Sum It Up!

① Mark It!

Draw an X on the animal that does not look like its young.

② Draw It!

Draw a picture of this animal's mother.

③ Solve It!

Answer the riddle.

I am little now.

I will change and grow.

Someday I will be an adult cat.

What am I? _____

④ Think About It!

Is a 👶 most like a 🐻 , a 🦎 , or a 🐛 ? Why?

Name _____

Word Play

Use these words to complete the puzzle.

tadpole   change   pupa   larva   reproduce   cycle

Across

1. The stage in a butterfly's life cycle after the egg

2. To make more living things of the same kind

Down

3. The stage in a butterfly's life between larva and adult

4. A young frog that lives in water

5. This takes place during metamorphosis in frogs and butterflies

6. All the stages of an animal's life make up its life _____.

Apply Concepts

How is the life cycle of a butterfly different from the life cycle of a polar bear? Use this chart to show your answer.

Life Cycles

Butterfly	Polar Bear
A butterfly hatches from an egg.	_____ _____
_____ _____	A polar bear cub drinks milk from its mother's body.
_____ _____	A polar bear cub looks a lot like its parents.
A butterfly larva does not stay with its parents.	_____ _____

Take It Home!

Family Members: Discuss life cycles with your child. Sort family photographs to show ways that your child and others have grown and changed over the years.

Learn About...
Salim Ali

Salim Ali is called the "Birdman of India." He traveled around India to study birds in their habitats. Ali discovered some kinds of birds. He wrote books about the birds he observed. Many people enjoyed reading his books.

Fun Fact

Bird watchers use binoculars like these to see birds more closely.

Watch the Bird Grow!

Salim Ali learned about birds. You can learn about birds, too.

▶ Order the life cycle of a robin. Number the pictures from 1 to 4.

_____ young robin

_____ adult robin

_____ robin chick

_____ robin eggs

▶ How is a robin's life cycle like the life cycles of other animals you know?

_____

_____

_____

_____

_____

_____

Essential Question

What Are Fossils?

Engage Your Brain!

Find the answer to the question in the lesson.

Dinosaurs do not live on Earth anymore. How do we learn about them?

We look at

_____ .

Active Reading

Lesson Vocabulary

1 Preview the lesson.

2 Write the 3 vocabulary terms here.

_____   _____

_____

Fossil Finds

These bones are from a dinosaur. A **dinosaur** was an animal that lived on Earth millions of years ago. Today, dinosaurs are extinct. **Extinct** is no longer living. So how do we know about dinosaurs?

bones of a *Tyrannosaurus rex*

drawing of a *Tyrannosaurus rex*

© Houghton Mifflin Harcourt Publishing Company (cl) ©Michele Falzone/Alamy; (c) ©Corbis; (bg) ©Robert Shantz/Alamy; (t) ©ROGER HARRIS/SPL/SPU/Getty Images; (inset)

fossil casts of shells

Scientists learn about dinosaurs from fossils. A **fossil** is what is left from a plant or animal that lived long ago. A fossil can be a footprint or an imprint in rock. A fossil can also be bones that have turned to rock.

fossil imprint of a fern

▶ A fern made this fossil. Draw what the fern may have looked like when it was alive.

Forming Fossils

Fossils form when plants and animals are buried under mud, clay, or sand. Follow the steps to see how this fossil formed.

▶ **Name the step that happened before the fossil was found.**

_____

First, the ammonite died. Mud and sand covered the ammonite.

Next, its soft body parts rotted away. Its hard shell remained.

ammonite
fossil

Then the mud, the sand, and the hard shell slowly turned to rock.

After millions of years, erosion removed the rock around the fossil. The fossil was found.

Fossil Clues

Fossils help scientists learn about living things from long ago. Scientists look at where fossils are found. They put fossil pieces together. They compare fossils of plants and animals to plants and animals that are living today. The fossils give clues about how extinct animals once looked, ate, and moved.

Active Reading

The main idea is the most important idea about something. Draw two lines under the main idea.

▶ We can learn about this once-living thing from its fossil. What did it eat?

_____

bones of a woolly mammoth

drawing of a woolly mammoth

▶ We can learn about a woolly mammoth from the environment where its fossil was found. The drawing shows fur. Why did the woolly mammoth need fur?

_____

Sum It Up!

① Circle It!

Circle the animal that is extinct.

② Match It!

Match the living thing to its fossil.

Name _____

Word Play

Write a word from the word bank on each line to complete the story.

| dinosaurs | fossils | extinct |

Have you ever been to a natural history museum? There you can learn about animals that are _____, or no longer living.

You can learn about _____.
They were animals that lived on Earth millions of years ago.

You may see _____, or what are left from plants and animals that lived long ago.

Some fossils are imprints of small plants.

Others are the bones of huge animals.

All of them are very cool!

Apply Concepts

Fill in the chart. Show how a fossil forms.

How a Fossil Forms

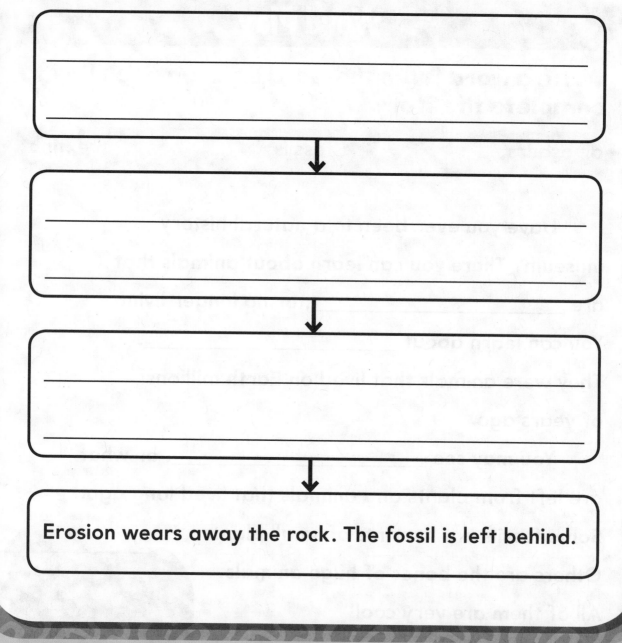

Erosion wears away the rock. The fossil is left behind.

Take It Home!

Name _____

Essential Question

How Can We Model a Fossil?

Set a Purpose

Write what you will do in this investigation.

_____

_____

Think About the Procedure

❶ What do you predict will happen when you press the shell into the clay?

_____

_____

❷ Why do you pour glue into the shell imprint?

_____

_____

Record Your Data

Draw and label pictures of each fossil model you made.

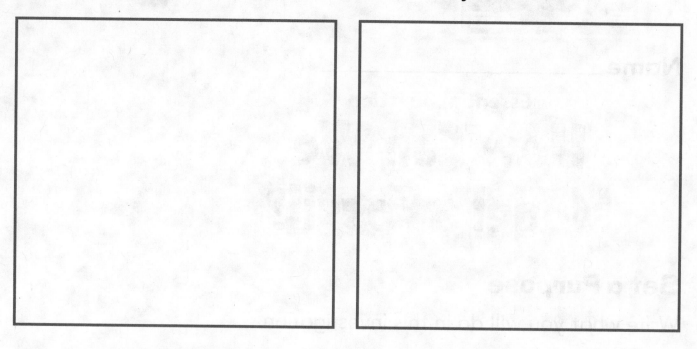

Draw Conclusions

What are two ways that fossils can form?

1 _____

_____

2 _____

_____

Ask More Questions

What other questions could you ask about fossils?

_____

_____

130

Unit 3 Review

Vocabulary Review

Use the terms in the box to complete the sentences.

> extinct
> shelter
> metamorphosis

1. Dinosaurs no longer live on Earth, so they are _____.

2. The changes an animal goes through are called _____.

3. An animal that has a safe place to live has _____.

Science Concepts

Fill in the letter of the choice that best answers the question.

4. How is a frog's life cycle the same as a bird's life cycle?
   - Ⓐ Both hatch from an egg.
   - Ⓑ Both go through metamorphosis.
   - Ⓒ Both look like their parents when they are born.

5. You see an animal that lays eggs. How can you tell if it is a bird?
   - Ⓐ find out if it can fly
   - Ⓑ find out if it has scales
   - Ⓒ find out if it has feathers

6. Which fish body part is **most** like the lungs of a cat?

   Ⓐ fins

   Ⓑ gills

   Ⓒ scales

7. What basic need is the animal meeting?

   Ⓐ the need for air

   Ⓑ the need for food

   Ⓒ the need for shelter

8. How do scientists learn about dinosaurs?

   Ⓐ They study fossils.

   Ⓑ They study living dinosaurs.

   Ⓒ They make living dinosaurs into fossils.

9. How do fins help fish?

   Ⓐ Fins help fish balance and steer.

   Ⓑ Fins help fish take in oxygen.

   Ⓒ Fins help fish lay eggs.

10. Which stage of the butterfly life cycle does this picture show?

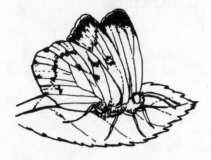

Ⓐ adult
Ⓑ larva
Ⓒ pupa

11. Which part of a mammal is **most likely** to become a fossil?

Ⓐ bones
Ⓑ fur
Ⓒ skin

12. This bird is hatching from an egg.

Which animal's life cycle is **most** similar to the bird's life cycle?

Ⓐ a bear
Ⓑ a dog
Ⓒ a turtle

UNIT 3

Inquiry and the Big Idea
Write the answers to these questions.

13. You want to know if this animal is a reptile or an amphibian.

What do you need to know to classify it?

_____

_____

14. Look at this fossil of a fish.

How did it form?

1. _____

2. _____

_____

3. _____

_____

All About Plants

Big Idea

All plants need certain things to live and grow. Plants have parts that help them grow.

sunflowers

I Wonder Why

The sunflowers all face the sun. Why?
Turn the page to find out.

Here's Why Plants, such as sunflowers, need sunlight to live. They face the sun to get as much sunlight as they can.

In this unit, you will explore this Big Idea, the Essential Questions, and the Investigations on the Inquiry Flipchart.

Levels of Inquiry Key ■ DIRECTED ■ GUIDED ■ INDEPENDENT

Track Your Progress

Big Idea All plants need certain things to live and grow. Plants have parts that help them grow.

Essential Questions

Lesson 1 What Are Plant Needs? 137
Inquiry Flipchart p. 18—Block the Light/Airtight Seal

S.T.E.M. Engineering and Technology: Bringing Water to Plants 145
Inquiry Flipchart p. 19—Compare It: Drip Tips

Inquiry Lesson 2 What Do Plants Need to Grow? 147
Inquiry Flipchart p. 20—What Do Plants Need to Grow?

Lesson 3 What Are Some Plant Parts? 149
Inquiry Flipchart p. 21—Plant Stems/Plant Parts

Lesson 4 What Are Some Plant Life Cycles? 159
Inquiry Flipchart p. 22—Bud a Spud!/Speedy Seed Race

Inquiry Lesson 5 How Does a Bean Plant Grow? 171
Inquiry Flipchart p. 23—How Does a Bean Plant Grow?

People in Science: Dr. Maria Elena Zavala 173

Unit 4 Review 175

Now I Get the Big Idea!

Science Notebook

Before you begin each lesson, be sure to write your thoughts about the Essential Question.

Essential Question

What Are Plant Needs?

Engage Your Brain!

Find the answer to the question in the lesson.

What do you know about a pumpkin this big?

Its

_____

were met.

Active Reading

Lesson Vocabulary

1 Preview the lesson.

2 Write the 2 vocabulary terms here.

_____ _____

Plant Needs

Plants are living things. All living things must have certain things to live and grow. These things are called **basic needs**. What happens if a plant does not meet its basic needs? It may stop growing. It may turn brown or begin to droop. It may die.

Circle details that tell what happens when a plant does not meet its basic needs.

These plants are meeting their basic needs.

▶ **What basic need is the boy giving the plants?**

Water

People can help plants meet their basic needs.

Wonderful Water

Plants need water. Do you know how they get it? A plant's roots take in water from the soil. Water is a basic need that helps plants live and grow.

Light and Airy

Do you wonder why people put some potted plants by windows? Plants need sunlight to grow. They also need air and water. Plants use air, water, and sunlight to make their own food.

Active Reading

Underline the sentence that tells what plants need to make food.

How are these plants getting what they need?

© Houghton Mifflin Harcourt Publishing Company   (bkgd) © BloomImage/Corbis

Nutrients and Space

Plants need nutrients from the soil. **Nutrients** are substances that help plants grow. Growing plants need more nutrients and water. Their roots grow and spread to get more of these things. Plants need enough space for their roots, stems, and leaves to grow.

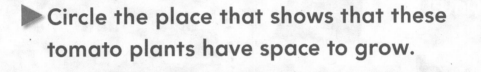

▶ **Circle the place that shows that these tomato plants have space to grow.**

Sum It Up!

1 Mark It!

Cross out the thing that a plant does not need to grow.

2 Solve It!

Fill in the blank.

I am all around you but you can't see me. I am something all living things need.

What am I?

_____

3 Draw It!

Draw a picture of a plant. Label the picture to show that the plant is getting what it needs.

Name _____

Word Play

Find and circle the words in this word search. Then answer the question.

| sunlight | water | soil | air | space | nutrients |

```
s  u  n  l  i  g  h  t  a  s
p  a  e  k  w  a  t  r  b  o
a  i  r  y  a  n  s  o  i  l
c  p  c  e  t  l  d  o  u  i
e  t  s  p  e  c  a  t  m  n
a  n  u  t  r  i  e  n  t  s
```

What are the things that plants must meet to live and grow?

_____

Complete the word web to tell about the things that plants need.

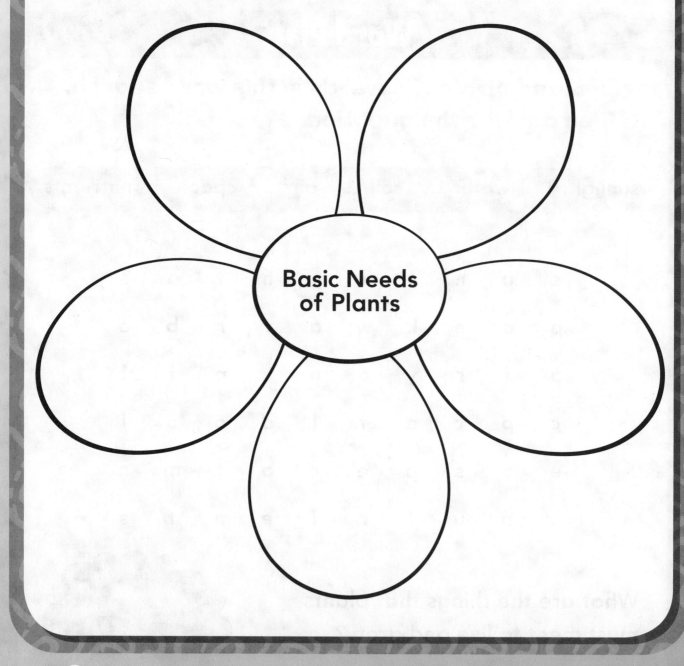

Basic Needs of Plants

Family Members: With your child, talk about the plants that grow in or around your home. Ask your child to tell how the plants get the things they need to grow.

Bringing Water to Plants

Drip Irrigation

Irrigation is a way to get water to land so plants can grow. A lawn sprinkler is one kind of irrigation.

Drip irrigation is another kind of irrigation. Hoses carry water to plants. Water drips from emitters on the hoses. This brings water right to the soil around the plants. Less water is wasted. Less water evaporates.

emitter

hose

Two Ways

Compare sprinkler irrigation and drip irrigation. Write a possible good thing and bad thing about each system.

Good _____

_____

Bad _____

_____

Good _____

_____

Bad _____

_____

Build On It!

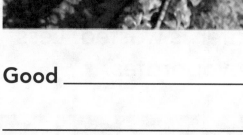

Compare different kinds of drip irrigation. Complete **Compare It: Drip Tips** on the Inquiry Flipchart.

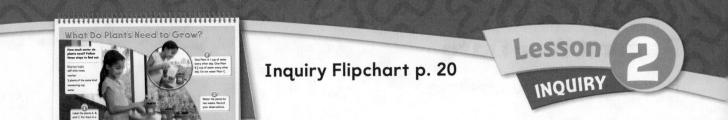

Name _____

Essential Question

What Do Plants Need to Grow?

Set a Purpose

Tell what you want to find out.

_____

_____

Think About the Procedure

1 What will you observe?

_____

_____

2 How will you treat the plants differently?

_____

_____

Record Your Data

Record what you observe.

My Observations			
Number of Days	Plant A	Plant B	Plant C
Day 2			
Day 5			
Day 7			
Day 10			

Draw Conclusions

❶ Do plants need water to grow? Tell how you know.

_____

❷ Can a plant get too much water? Explain.

_____

Ask More Questions

What are some other questions about what plants need to grow?

_____

_____

_____

148

Essential Question

What Are Some Plant Parts?

Engage Your Brain!

Find the answer to the question in the lesson.

This flower smells bad to attract insects.

Why do flowers attract insects?

_____

Active Reading

Lesson Vocabulary

1 Preview the lesson.

2 Write the 3 vocabulary terms here.

_____ _____

_____

A Part to Play

Plants need sunlight, air, water, and nutrients from the soil to grow. Each part of a plant helps the plant get what it needs to live and grow.

Flowers, leaves, stems, and roots are important parts of a plant. Find these parts in the picture.

Active Reading

The main idea is the most important idea about something. Draw two lines under the main idea.

▶ Circle the stem.
Mark an X on the flower.
Draw a box around a leaf.

flower

leaf

stem

roots

Do the Job

Flowers help plants make new plants. Parts of a flower make seeds that grow into new plants.

Leaves make food for the plant. They use air, water, and sunlight to make the food.

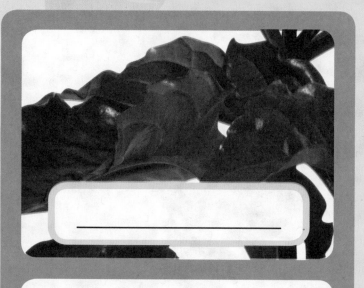

▶ Write a label on each line to name the plant part in the picture.

_____

Stems carry water and nutrients from the roots to the leaves and other parts of the plant. They also hold up the plant.

_____

The roots grow into the soil and hold the plant in place. They take in water and nutrients from the soil.

Flower Power

The plant part that makes seeds is the flower. The flower has its own parts, too. Some parts of a flower are pollen, petals, and seeds.

Active Reading

A detail is a fact about a main idea. Draw one line under a detail. Draw an arrow to the main idea it tells about.

Flowers make pollen. **Pollen** is a powder that flowers need to make seeds. Most plants use pollen from other flowers to make seeds. Insects, animals, and wind may carry pollen from one flower to another.

The colorful petals attract insects and animals. A plant may need insects and animals to move pollen.

Flowers make seeds. A new plant may grow from a **seed**.

▶ What part of a plant grows into a new plant?

_____

Sum It Up!

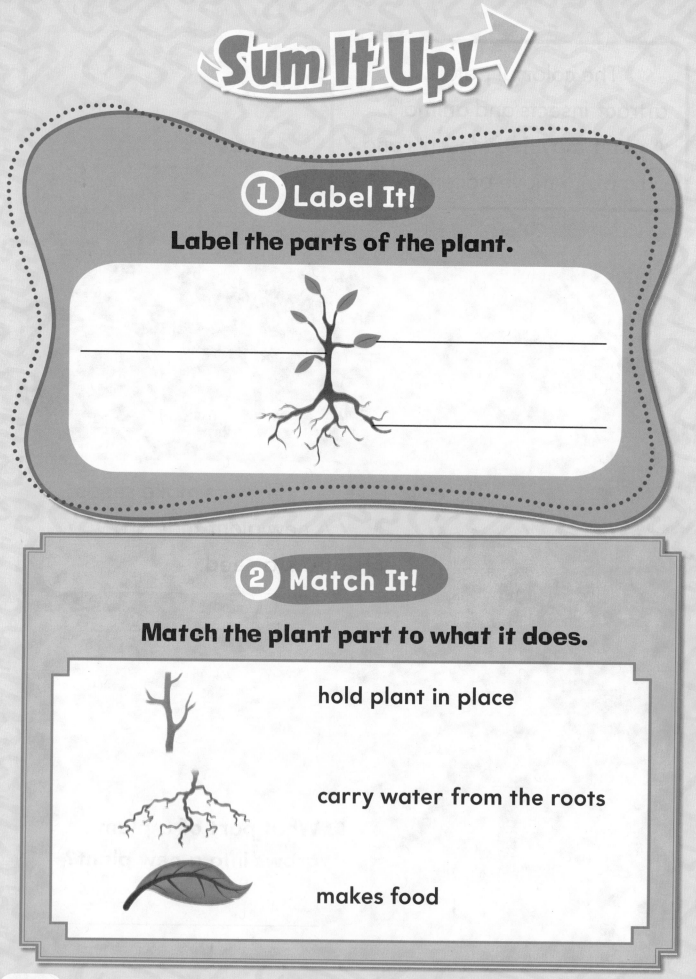

1 Label It!

Label the parts of the plant.

2 Match It!

Match the plant part to what it does.

hold plant in place

carry water from the roots

makes food

Name _____

Word Play

Read the clues. Use the words to complete the puzzle.

leaf   stem   flower   seed   roots   pollen

Across

1. plant part that makes food
2. take in water from the soil
3. carries water from the roots

Down

4. powder that helps make seeds
5. plant part with petals
6. grows into new plants

Apply Concepts

Fill in the chart. Write the name of the plant part or what the plant part does.

Plant Parts

Part	What It Does
_____	carries water and nutrients from the roots to other plant parts
roots	_____ _____
pollen	_____ _____
_____	makes seeds

Family Members: Ask your child to observe plants at home, in a garden, or in your neighborhood. Have your child identify the roots, stem, leaves, and flowers, and describe what each plant part does.

Take It Home!

Essential Question

What Are Some Plant Life Cycles?

Engage Your Brain!

Find the answer to the question in this lesson.

What does the flower part of a dandelion make?

It makes

_____ .

Active Reading

Lesson Vocabulary

1. Preview the lesson.
2. Write the 4 vocabulary terms here.

_____   _____

_____   _____

Plant Start-Ups

Plants are living things. They grow and change. They have life cycles. Most plant life cycles begin with a **seed**. New plants grow from seeds. The growing plants start to look like their parent plants.

Active Reading

Find the words that tell about seeds. Draw a line under the words.

The plants in this garden grew from seeds.

How Fast Do Plants Grow?

Some plants grow quickly. Plants in a vegetable garden take just a few months to become adult plants. Other plants, such as trees, take many years to become adults.

Do the Math!

Interpret a Table

Use the chart to answer the question.

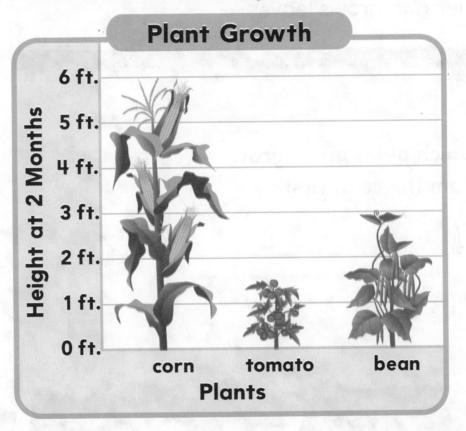

Plant Growth

Height at 2 Months: 6 ft., 5 ft., 4 ft., 3 ft., 2 ft., 1 ft., 0 ft.

Plants: corn, tomato, bean

▶ How much taller did the corn plant grow than the bean plant?

Start with a Seed

What happens when you plant a seed? When a seed gets warmth, air, and water, it may germinate. **Germinate** means to start to grow. The stem of the tiny plant breaks through the ground. The plant gets taller and grows leaves.

▶ Which plant parts grow from the seed first?

_____

A tiny plant is inside a seed.

The seed germinates. The roots grow down.

The stem grows up toward the light.

Growing Up

The tiny plant inside the seed has become a young plant called a **seedling**.

The seedling grows into an adult plant. An adult plant can make flowers and seeds.

Active Reading

Find the words that tell the meaning of **seedling**. Draw a line under those words.

The plant grows more roots and leaves.

The adult plant grows flowers.

Apples
All Around

Some plants have flowers that make seeds and fruit. Parts of the flower grow into fruit. The fruit grows around the seeds to hold and protect them.

Active Reading

Circle the word **seeds** each time you see it on these two pages.

apple blossoms

Parts of apple blossoms grow into apples. The apples grow around seeds.

A Long Life

Some plants have short lives. They die soon after their flowers make seeds. Other plants, such as apple trees, can live for many years. An apple tree can live for a hundred years or more!

adult apple tree

▶ **What do apple blossoms make?**

Inside a Cone

Some plants, like pine trees, do not have flowers. But they do have seeds. Where do their seeds grow? A **cone** is a part of a pine tree and some other plants. Seeds grow inside the cone.

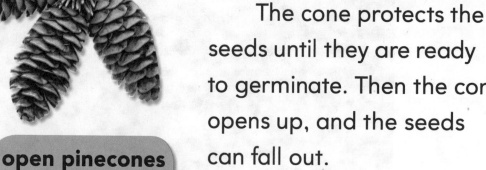

closed pinecones

open pinecones with seeds

The cone protects the seeds until they are ready to germinate. Then the cone opens up, and the seeds can fall out.

▶ **Where do pine seeds form?**

Pine Tree Beginnings

Pine seeds fall to the ground and germinate. As the seedlings grow, they start to look like their parent plants. After a few years, the pine trees grow cones and make seeds. The life cycle begins again.

adult pine trees

▶ What happens after an adult pine tree grows cones and makes seeds?

_____

_____

Sum It Up!

① Draw It!

Draw the missing step in the plant's life cycle. Label your picture.

seed   _____   seedling   adult

② Mark It!

Draw an X on the plant part that does not have seeds.

③ Think About It!

How are flowers and pinecones alike?

_____

_____

Name _____

Word Play

Read each word. Trace a path through the maze to connect each word to its picture.

seed	cone	flower	seedling

Write to tell about the life cycle of a plant. Use the words <u>germinate</u>, <u>seed</u>, and <u>seedling</u>.

Life Cycle of a Plant

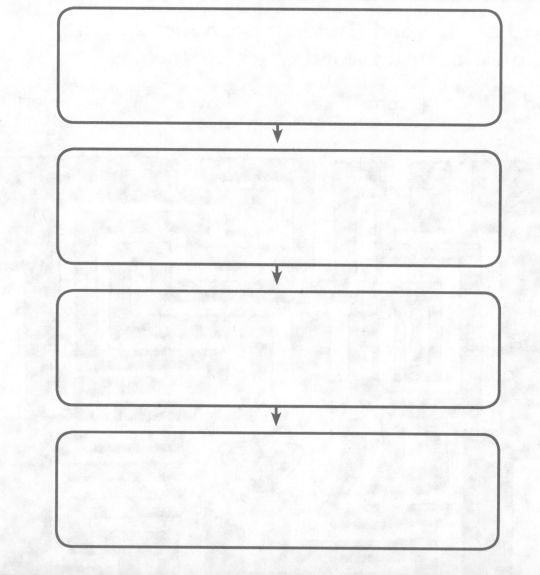

Take It Home!

Family Members: Ask your child to tell you about plant life cycles. Then take a walk around your neighborhood. Talk about the plants you see.

Name _____

How Does a Bean Plant Grow?

Set a Purpose

Explain what you will learn from this activity.

_____

_____

Think About the Procedure

❶ Why must you give the plant water and sunlight?

_____

_____

❷ Compare the way that your bean plant grew with the way that a classmate's bean plant grew. What was the same?

_____

_____

_____

Record Your Data

In this chart, record what you observe.

Date	Observations

Draw Conclusions

How did the bean plant change?

_____

_____

_____

Ask More Questions

What other questions could you ask about how plants grow?

_____

_____

Get to Know ...

Dr. Maria Elena Zavala

As a young girl, Maria Elena Zavala thought a lot about plants. Her grandmother lived next door. She grew plants to use as medicine. Young Maria learned about those plants from her grandmother.

Today Maria Elena Zavala is a botanist and a teacher. A botanist is a scientist who studies plants. Dr. Zavala studies how plants respond to their environment. She and her students are finding out how roots grow.

Fun Fact

As a child, Maria took apart her father's roses to learn more about plants.

173

Now You Be a Botanist!

▶ Draw and label roots, flowers, and leaves on this plant.

Unit 4 Review

Vocabulary Review

Use the terms in the box to complete the sentences.

| nutrients |
| pollen |
| seed |

1. Most plants grow from a _____.

2. Substances from soil that help plants grow are _____.

3. The powder that flowers need to make seeds is called _____.

Science Concepts

Fill in the letter of the choice that best answers the question.

4. Which does a plant use to make its own food?
   - Ⓐ pollen
   - Ⓑ seeds
   - Ⓒ water

5. Which plant part makes seeds?
   - Ⓐ flower
   - Ⓑ leaves
   - Ⓒ roots

6. Which part of the plant life cycle does this picture show?

(A) adult plant

(B) seed

(C) seedling

7. How are roots and stems alike?

(A) They hold up a plant.

(B) They can move nutrients.

(C) They keep a plant in soil.

8. Tina does an experiment with two plants of the same kind. She gives Plant 1 fresh water. She gives Plant 2 salt water. The pictures show the results of Tina's experiment.

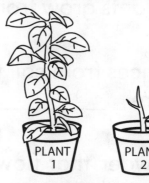

What can you infer?

(A) These plants grow better with salt water than with fresh water.

(B) These plants grow better with fresh water than with salt water.

(C) These plants grow the same with either fresh water or salt water.

9. Where does a plant get nutrients?

(A) from air

(B) from seeds

(C) from soil

10. How do you know that this plant is an adult plant?

Ⓐ The plant has roots.
Ⓑ The plant has leaves.
Ⓒ The plant has a flower.

11. What does a cone do?
Ⓐ A cone grows fruit.
Ⓑ A cone holds seeds.
Ⓒ A cone makes pollen.

12. Three identical plants were planted at the same time. Which one grew **fastest**?

Ⓐ the one on the left
Ⓑ the one in the middle
Ⓒ the one on the right

Inquiry and the Big Idea
Write the answers to these questions.

13. Look at this plant.

How does water move through the plant? How is water used in the different parts of the plant?

_____

_____

14. Tell how you would plan an investigation to show that plants need water to survive.

_____

_____

_____

_____

UNIT 5
Environments for Living Things

Big Idea

Living things meet their needs in their environments.

impala and red-billed oxpecker

I Wonder Why
The bird is picking bugs off the impala. Why?
Turn the page to find out.

Here's Why The bird eats the bugs for food.

In this unit, you will explore this Big Idea, the Essential Questions, and the Investigations on the Inquiry Flipchart.

Levels of Inquiry Key ■ DIRECTED ■ GUIDED ■ INDEPENDENT

Track Your Progress

Big Idea Living things meet their needs in their environments.

Essential Questions

Lesson 1 How Do Plants and Animals Need One Another?.......................... 181
Inquiry Flipchart p. 24—Helpful Plants/Model a Food Chain

Lesson 2 How Are Living Things Adapted to Their Environments?..................... 193
Inquiry Flipchart p. 25—Design a Bird/Waxy Leaves

Inquiry Lesson 3 Can Plants Survive in Different Environments?..................... 205
Inquiry Flipchart p. 26—Can Plants Survive in Different Environments?

S.T.E.M. Engineering and Technology: Technology and the Environment.................... 207
Inquiry Flipchart p. 27—Design It: Water Filter

Lesson 4 How Do Environments Change Over Time?....................... 209
Inquiry Flipchart p. 28—Flood!/Plan to Help

🌎 Careers in Science: Environmental Scientist........ 219

Unit 5 Review................................. 221

Now I Get the Big Idea!

Science Notebook

Before you begin each lesson, be sure to write your thoughts about the Essential Question.

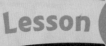

Essential Question

How Do Plants and Animals Need One Another?

🧠 Engage Your Brain!

Find the answer to the question in the lesson.

This bat drinks from the plant. How is the bat also helping the plant?

The bat spreads

_____ .

Active Reading

Lesson Vocabulary

1 Preview the lesson.

2 Write the 3 vocabulary terms here.

_____   _____

_____

In Your Place

Plants and animals use living and nonliving things to meet their needs. They get the things they need from their environment. All the living and nonliving things in a place make up an **environment**.

Active Reading

Find the sentence that tells the meaning of **environment**. Draw a line under the sentence.

Plants and animals need water.

Plants and animals need air.

Plants need sunlight to make food. Animals find food in their environment.

Plants and animals need space to live and grow. Animals find shelter in the environment where they live.

▶ What do both plants and animals need from their environment?

_____

_____

Getting Help

Animals use plants to meet their needs. Many animals use plants for shelter. Some animals hide in plants. Other animals live in plants or use them to build homes.

Active Reading

A detail is a fact about a main idea. Draw one line under a detail. Draw an arrow to the main idea it tells about.

An owl finds shelter in a tree.

A lion hides in tall grass.

Animals need to breathe air to get oxygen, a gas in the air. Plants give off oxygen. Some animals use plants for food. Some animals eat animals that eat plants.

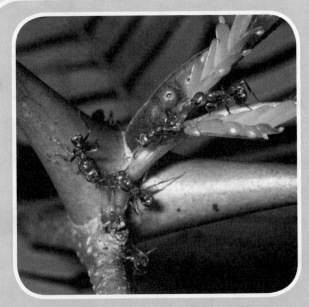

Ants find both food and shelter in the thorns of this tree.

A panda eats bamboo.

▶ Write another example of how an animal uses plants to meet its needs.

_____

_____

_____

_____

Giving Help

Animals may help plants reproduce, or make new plants. Some animals carry fruits to new places. There, the seeds inside the fruits may grow into new plants.

Active Reading

The main idea is the most important idea about something. Draw two lines under the main idea.

The dog spreads seeds that are inside the burrs on its fur.

Some animals spread pollen for plants. **Pollen** is a powder that flowers need to make seeds. Pollen may stick to an animal. The animal carries the pollen from flower to flower. This helps plants make new plants.

As a bat drinks the flower nectar, pollen rubs off on the bat.

A woodpecker moves acorns with its beak. Seeds are inside the acorns.

A beetle carries pollen on its body.

▶ Underline two examples of how animals help plants reproduce.

Eat Up!

These pictures show a food chain. A **food chain** shows how energy moves from plants to animals. Follow the arrows. They show how plants and animals are linked in a food chain.

Food chains start with sunlight and plants. In this food chain, the water plants use sunlight to make food.

An eagle eats the turtle.

A turtle eats the water plants.

▶ Draw what is missing from the first step of the food chain.

Sum It Up!

① Label It!

Write <u>water</u>, <u>food</u>, or <u>shelter</u> to tell what each living thing is getting from its environment.

_____   _____
          _____   _____

② Order It!

Number the steps in this food chain to show the correct order.

_____   _____   _____

Name _____

Word Play

Read each clue below. Then unscramble the letters to write the correct answer.

environment   oxygen   pollen   food chain

1. a gas in the air that animals need to survive

   nxyego   _____

2. all the living and nonliving things in a place

   nervnitnmeo   _____

3. shows how energy moves from plants to animals

   ofod   inhca   _____

4. flowers need this to make seeds

   lonpel   _____

Apply Concepts

Use words from the word bank to complete the chart.

| shelter | oxygen | seeds | food | pollen |

Ways Animals Use Plants	Ways Animals Help Plants
When animals build nests, they use plants for _____.	Animals help carry _____ to new places.
Animals eat plants as _____.	Animals spread _____ that sticks to their bodies.
Animals need _____ that plants give off.	

Family Members: Take a walk outside with your child. Help your child observe animals using plants.

Take It Home!

Essential Question

How Are Living Things Adapted to Their Environments?

Engage Your Brain!

Find the answer to the question in the lesson.

Find the caterpillar. How do its color and shape help it stay safe?

They help it

_____.

Active Reading

Lesson Vocabulary

1 Preview the lesson.

2 Write the vocabulary term here.

_____

Survival Skills

Plants live almost everywhere. Some places they live are dry. Other places are wet and shady. Plants have ways to survive where they live. These ways are called adaptations. An **adaptation** is something that helps a living thing survive in its environment.

Water lilies have long stems that let their leaves reach the water's surface. There, the leaves get sunlight.

► Look at this plant. Circle the kind of environment where it would best survive.

dry   wet

Cacti live where it is dry. Their thick, waxy stems store water.

Rain forest plants have very large leaves. These leaves help the plants get sunlight in the shady forest.

Animals At Home

Animals also have adaptations to help them survive in their environments. They may live where there is little food. They may live where it is very cold. Their adaptations help them survive where they live.

Active Reading

The main idea is the most important idea about something. Draw two lines under the main idea.

Camels live where it is dry and sandy. Long eyelashes help keep sand out of their eyes.

Penguins live on ice and in cold water. A thick layer of fat keeps them warm.

Giraffes have long tongues to pull leaves off trees.

▶ Look at this animal. Circle the kind of environment where it would best survive.

dry, sandy

cold water

Plant Protection

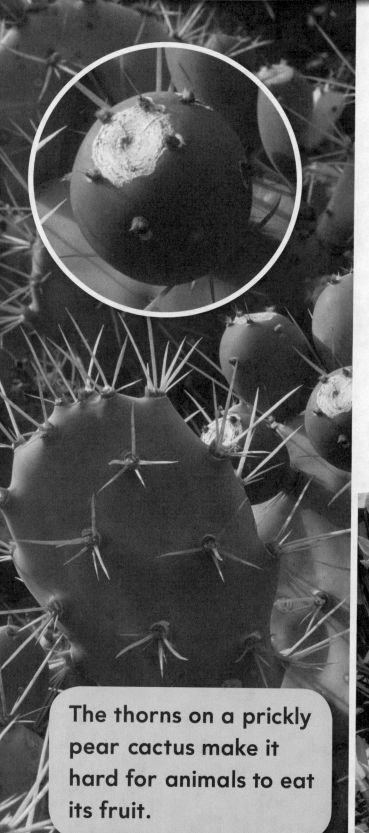

Living things also have adaptations to protect themselves. Plant adaptations help keep plants safe from animals that might eat them. Some of these adaptations are thorns, bad taste, and quick movement.

Daffodils taste bad. Animals do not like to eat them.

The thorns on a prickly pear cactus make it hard for animals to eat its fruit.

The leaves of the mimosa plant fold quickly when touched. This may knock off insects that want to eat the leaves.

▶ Name two plant adaptations that protect plants from animals.

_____

_____

_____

_____

Animal Protection

Many animals must protect themselves from other animals. They have adaptations to help them stay safe. These adaptations help protect animals from other animals that want to eat them.

Active Reading

A detail is a fact about a main idea. Draw one line under a detail. Draw an arrow to the main idea it tells about.

Skunks can spray a bad smell. The bad smell scares off other animals.

Sea urchins have long, sharp spines. The spines protect them from fish and crabs.

▶ Write two characteristics that help the leaf insect survive.

_____

_____

The leaf insect looks like the leaf. This helps the insect hide.

Sum It Up!

① Match It!

Match each living thing to the environment where it lives.

cold, snowy   dry, sandy   wet, shady

② Write It!

Write how each living thing protects itself.

_____   _____   _____

Name _____

Word Play

Define the word adaptation. Then list adaptations that help plants and animals survive.

adaptation:

_____

_____

Plants	Animals
large leaves	fat
_____	_____
_____	_____
_____	_____
_____	_____
_____	_____

Apply Concepts

Write two details that go with the main idea.
Include details about two different adaptations.

Main Idea
Adaptations help living things survive in different environments.

Detail	Detail
_____	_____
_____	_____
_____	_____
_____	_____
_____	_____

Family Members: Ask your child to describe some animal adaptations. Discuss how those adaptations help the animals survive.

Name _____

Essential Question

Can Plants Survive in Different Environments?

Set a Purpose

Write what you want to find out.

_____

_____

Make a Prediction

Write a prediction about what you think will happen.

_____

_____

Think About the Procedure

❶ Why will you water the **desert** plant only once?

_____

❷ Why will you water the **rain forest** plant three times a day?

_____

205

Record Your Data

In this chart, record what you observe.

Date	Desert Plant	Rain Forest Plant

Draw Conclusions

Was your prediction right? Can a plant from one environment live in a different environment? How do you know?

_____

_____

Ask More Questions

What other questions could you ask about plants in different environments?

_____

_____

Technology and the Environment

Dams

A dam is a wall built across a river. It slows the flow of the river. A dam can be helpful. It can provide water for drinking. It can provide water for crops. It can also control floods.

A dam can also harm the environment. Fish, like salmon, cannot migrate across some dams. Some animals lose their homes when a dam is built.

salmon migrating

Helpful and Harmful

How are dams helpful? How are dams harmful? Use your ideas to complete the chart.

Effects of Dams	
Helpful	**Harmful**

Build On It!

Learn more about water and technology. Complete **Design It: Water Filter** on the Inquiry Flipchart.

Essential Question

How Do Environments Change Over Time?

🧠 Engage Your Brain!

Find the answer to the question in the lesson.

What changed this environment?

_____

Active Reading

Lesson Vocabulary

1. Preview the lesson.

2. Write the vocabulary term here.

_____

Nature's Work

Things happen in nature that can change environments over time. Different kinds of weather change an environment from season to season. Fires and earthquakes can make changes in minutes.

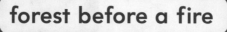

forest before a fire

Fire can change an environment. It burns trees and plants. Some animals move to safer places. Some animals may die.

The changes do not last forever. New trees and plants grow back. Animals come back to the area to live in the trees and eat the plants.

Active Reading

A cause tells why something happens. Draw one line under a cause.

forest during a fire

▶ **Name an effect of fire on an environment.**

_____

_____

A Change of Pace

Animals and plants can change an environment. The kudzu plant grows very fast. The plant will grow over other plants. The plants that are covered do not get enough light. They may die.

Beavers build dams, which form ponds. Beavers pile sticks, branches, and mud over a shallow area of running water. The dam blocks the running water and makes a pond.

When beavers cut down trees, some birds and insects lose their homes.

A kudzu plant has grown over these cars.

The pond that beavers make becomes a home for some plants and animals.

Do the Math!

Skip Count by 10s

A beaver dam can be 10 feet high! How high would 3 beaver dams be? Skip count to find the answer. Show your work.

_____ feet

What People Do

People change environments, too. People change environments because they need resources. A **resource** is anything people can use to meet their needs. People can help and harm environments. How do you change your environment?

Active Reading

Find the sentence that tells the meaning of **resource**. Draw a line under the sentence.

Pollution and trash harm environments.

Reducing trash and recycling help keep environments clean.

People may need to cut down trees to make space for buildings.

People help by planting new trees.

▶ Write how people can change the environment.

help	harm

Sum It Up!

1 Match It!

Match each thing to the way it changes its environment.

burns trees

grows over
other plants

builds dams

2 Circle It!

Circle the ways that people can help an environment.

recycle   waste resources   plant trees

Name _____

Word Play

Draw lines to match each word to its description.

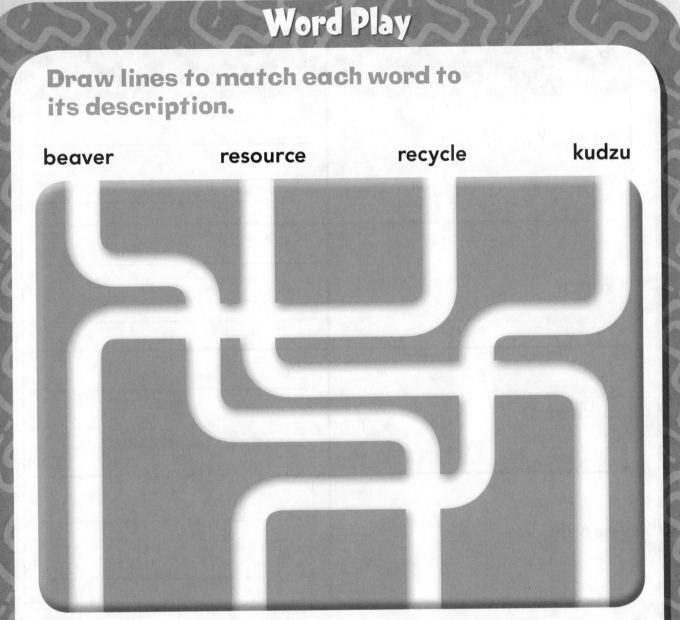

beaver   resource   recycle   kudzu

anything people can use to meet their needs

an animal that builds dams

a plant that grows over other plants

to use old resources to make new things

Apply Concepts

Fill in the chart. Write how each thing can change its environment.

How Environments Change

Things That Change Environments	How They Change Environments
fire	_____ _____
kudzu	_____ _____
beaver	_____ _____
people	_____ _____

Take It Home!

Family Members: Walk with your child through your neighborhood. Observe and discuss ways that living things and other things that happen in nature have changed the environment.

Ask an Environmental Scientist

What do environmental scientists do?

We study the harmful effects to different kinds of environments.

How do environmental scientists help wildlife?

We find problems that affect wildlife and people in the environments. We figure out ways to solve those problems.

Sometimes people can harm an environment. For example, a factory may put waste into a stream. This may kill fish. We help the factory find other ways to get rid of its waste.

Now It's Your Turn!

▶ What question would you ask an environmental scientist?

_____

_____

_____

Making Environments Better

▶ Draw or write the answer to each question.

1 What do you think is most interesting about what environmental scientists do?

2 What might be difficult about what they do?

3 Why are environmental scientists important?

4 Think about being an environmental scientist. Draw an environment you would like to study.

1

_____

_____

_____

2

_____

_____

3

_____

_____

4

Unit 5 Review

Vocabulary Review

Use the terms in the box to complete the sentences.

> adaptation
> food chain
> resource

1. A(n) _____ shows how energy moves from plants to animals.

2. Anything that people can use to meet their needs is a(n) _____.

3. Humps help camels survive in their environment. Humps are a(n) _____.

Science Concepts

Fill in the letter of the choice that best answers the question.

4. Which is an example of a natural event changing a forest?
   - (A) a forest fire
   - (B) people planting trees
   - (C) people cutting down trees

5. How are the needs of plants and animals alike?
   - (A) Animals and plants both need sunlight to make their own food.
   - (B) Animals and plants both need air and water to survive.
   - (C) Animals and plants both need lungs to breathe.

6. This picture shows the steps in a food chain.

Which statement about this food chain is **true**?

Ⓐ Frogs eat grasshoppers.

Ⓑ Grasshoppers eat frogs.

Ⓒ Frogs and grasshoppers eat each other.

7. A plant has adaptations for living in a wet, shady environment. What will **most likely** happen if it is moved to a sunny, dry place?

Ⓐ The plant will die.

Ⓑ The plant will grow better.

Ⓒ The plant will grow as well.

8. What is the main reason people make changes to environments?

Ⓐ They need resources.

Ⓑ They have bad adaptations.

Ⓒ They want to help the environment.

9. Which begins every food chain?

Ⓐ plants

Ⓑ turtles

Ⓒ sunlight and plants

10. How do animals help plants meet their needs?

   Ⓐ by making food for them

   Ⓑ by spreading their seeds and pollen

   Ⓒ by giving them shelter and oxygen

11. Look at the adaptations of this polar bear.

Where would the bear best survive?

   Ⓐ hot, dry environment

   Ⓑ cold, icy environment

   Ⓒ warm, wet environment

12. Plants may change an environment over time. Which of these things can **most** change an environment in minutes?

   Ⓐ animals

   Ⓑ fire

   Ⓒ soil

Inquiry and the Big Idea
Write the answers to these questions.

13. Describe two adaptations that would help an animal survive in a cold environment. Explain your answer.

_____

_____

14. Suppose a fire changes an environment. How will you know if a plant living in the environment has the adaptations to survive in the new environment?

_____

_____

_____

UNIT 6
Earth and Its Resources

Big Idea

Changes can occur to Earth's surface. People need Earth resources like rock, plants, and water.

Fort Jefferson, Florida Keys

I Wonder Why
People use materials from Earth to build things. Why?
Turn the page to find out.

Here's Why Materials such as rock are easy to find. They also last a long time and are strong enough to build things.

In this unit, you will explore this Big Idea, the Essential Questions, and the Investigations on the Inquiry Flipchart.

Levels of Inquiry Key ■ DIRECTED ■ GUIDED ■ INDEPENDENT

Track Your Progress

Big Idea Changes can occur to Earth's surface. People need Earth resources like rock, plants, and water.

Essential Questions

Lesson 1 What Changes Earth? 227
Inquiry Flipchart p. 29—Earth Shake/Erosion Made Easy

Careers in Science: Geologist 239

Lesson 2 What Are Natural Resources? 241
Inquiry Flipchart p. 30—Looking at Lunch/Product Hunt

S.T.E.M. **Engineering and Technology:**
How It's Made: Cotton Shirt 253
Inquiry Flipchart p. 31—Test It: Strong Buildings

**Inquiry Lesson 3 How Can We Classify Plant
Products?** 255
Inquiry Flipchart p. 32—How Can We Classify Plant Products?

Unit 6 Review 259

Now I Get the Big Idea!

Science Notebook

Before you begin each lesson, be sure to write your thoughts about the Essential Question.

Essential Question

What Changes Earth?

🧠 Engage Your Brain!

Find the answer to the question in the lesson.

What changed the shape of these rocks over time?

_____

Active Reading

Lesson Vocabulary

1 Preview the lesson.

2 Write the 6 vocabulary terms here.

_____ _____

_____ _____

_____ _____

Make It Fast

Earth is always changing. Some changes are fast. They happen in minutes, hours, or days.

An earthquake is a fast change. An **earthquake** is a shaking of Earth's surface. Floods and eruptions from volcanoes are fast changes, too. A **volcano** is a place where hot melted rock comes out of the ground.

Active Reading

When things are compared, you find out ways they are alike. Draw triangles around two things that are being compared.

earthquake

ishing Company (tc) ©Douglas Peebles/Corbis; (bc) ©Michael S. Yamashita/Corbis

If a lot of rain falls, it can cause a flood. A **flood** happens when streams, rivers, or lakes overflow. The water flows onto land. The land is washed away to new places.

flood

volcano erupting

▶ Circle the labels that name fast changes.

Take It Slow

Some changes to Earth are slow. Slow changes happen over many months or years. Weathering is a slow change. **Weathering** happens when wind and water break down rock into smaller pieces. Erosion is also a slow change. **Erosion** happens when wind and water move rocks and soil. It changes the shape of land.

Active Reading

Draw one line under a detail. Draw an arrow to the main idea it tells about.

Erosion wears away the cliff.

drought

A drought is another slow change.
A **drought** is a long time with very little rain.
The land gets very dry. Streams and ponds
may dry up. Wind may blow away the soil.

Weathering and
erosion have worn
down these rocks.

▶ Can a drought last for
minutes or for years?

_____

Stop It!

Trees and other plants can help stop erosion. Their branches and leaves stop wind from blowing soil away.

Roots grow down into the soil and hold it in place. Then water cannot wash the soil away.

These trees hold soil in place and help stop erosion.

Look at the hillside. What happened? Trees were cut down. Now there are no branches or leaves to stop wind from blowing soil away. The dead roots cannot hold the soil in place.

▶ Draw a way to help stop erosion on this hillside.

Make a Match

Look at the **Before** and **After** pictures.
Make three matches to tell how Earth changes.

▶ Write the number of a Before picture on the After picture that matches.

Before

1

wall arch

2

land

3

Mount Saint Helens

After

weathering

volcano

flood

Sum It Up!

① Circle It!

Look at each picture. Then circle the effect.

Trees dry out.
Trees are burned.

Soil washes away.
Soil stays in place.

② Draw It!

Draw two changes to Earth. Label each fast or slow.

 **Brain Check**

Name _____

Word Play

Fill in the puzzle. Use these words.
Use the pictures to help.

earthquake   flood   drought   volcano   erosion

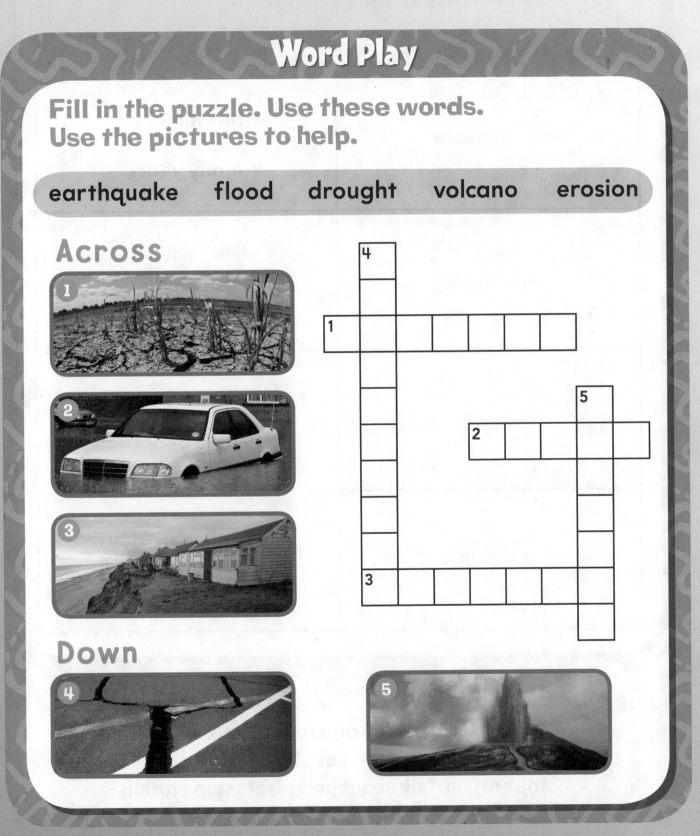

Across

1.
2.
3.

Down

4.
5.

Apply Concepts

Think about each change. Circle how much time you think it may take to happen.

Kind of Change	Time It May Take
earthquake	few minutes many years
weathering	few minutes many years
flood	few hours or days many years
erosion	few hours or days many years

Take It Home!

Family Members: Go on a nature walk with your child. Ask your child to point out places where plants help stop erosion. Talk about how plants stop erosion.

Ask a Geologist

What is a geologist?

A geologist is a scientist who studies Earth. We study the materials on Earth, such as rocks, soil, and water.

How do geologists work?

Some geologists dig up rocks. They work outside with hiking shoes and picks. Others stay in a lab. They use machines to collect and study data about Earth.

How does your work help people?

Geologists find water, oil, and gas underground. These are resources people need. We also study earthquakes and volcanoes to help people stay safe.

Now It's Your Turn!

▶ What question would you ask a geologist?

_____

_____

Tools of the Trade

▶ How do you think each tool helps a geologist?
Write your answers.

helmet

_____

_____

_____

_____

pick

_____

_____

_____

_____

compass

_____

_____

_____

_____

Essential Question

What Are Natural Resources?

Engage Your Brain!

Find the answer to the question in the lesson.

Look at the statues. What natural resource are they made from?

They are made from _____ .

Active Reading

Lesson Vocabulary

1. Preview the lesson.

2. Write the 2 vocabulary terms here.

_____ _____

It's Natural!

A **natural resource** is anything from nature that people can use. Some important natural resources are rocks, soil, water, and air.

Active Reading

Find the sentence that tells the meaning of **natural resource**. Draw a line under the sentence.

People use rocks to make buildings, roads, and walls.

People use soil to grow plants. Soil has nutrients and water that plants need to grow.

People breathe
air to live.

People drink water.
They also use it to cook,
bathe, and clean.

▶ Draw a way that people use water.

It's Second Nature

Animals and plants are important natural resources, too. They come from nature, and people can use them. Look at how people use animals and plants.

Some people use animals for food and clothing. They eat eggs from chickens. They use wool from sheep to make warm clothes.

People use plants for food. They also use plants to make and build things. Wood and cotton come from plants.

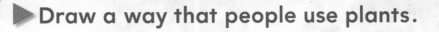

▶Draw a way that people use plants.

Product Power

Natural resources can be made into products. A **product** is something made by people or machines for people to use.

Natural Resource

wheat

cereal

cotton

_____

_____

pencils

▶ Complete the chart. Draw a natural resource or product in each empty box. Then write a label.

Products

pasta

_____

towels

first aid supplies

paper

furniture

Growing Up

In 1860, Seattle was a small town. Today it is a large city.

Trees grew well near Seattle. People went to Seattle to make the trees into products such as furniture and houses. This brought jobs and money to the town. Jobs and money helped the town grow.

The Great Seattle Fire burned many buildings. More people moved to Seattle after the fire. They took jobs to help rebuild the city.

Seattle, 1860

Natural resources can affect how an area grows. Trees brought jobs and money to Seattle. This helped Seattle grow.

Do the Math!

Solve a Problem

Use the timeline to solve the problem.

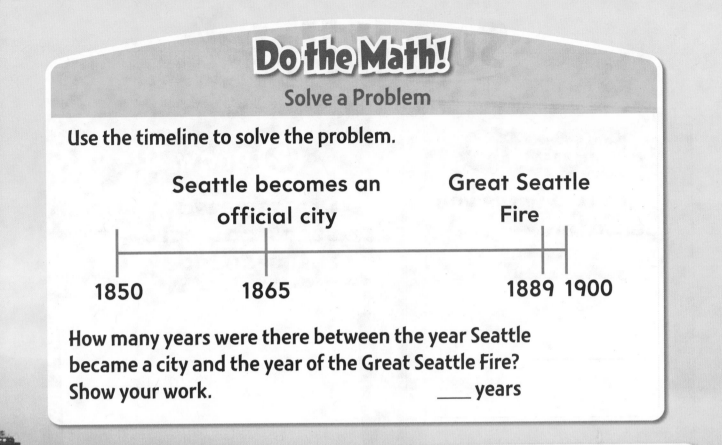

Seattle becomes an official city

Great Seattle Fire

1850   1865   1889 1900

How many years were there between the year Seattle became a city and the year of the Great Seattle Fire? Show your work.

_____ years

Today Seattle is a large city with bright lights and tall buildings.

Sum It Up!

① Write It!

Write two ways you use water.

_____

_____

_____

② Draw It!

Draw one way you used a natural resource today.

③ Circle It!

Circle the products that come from plants.

Name _____

Word Play

Write the definitions.

natural resource:

_____

_____

_____

product:

_____

_____

_____

Match each natural resource to its product.

Apply Concepts

Fill in the chart. Show how plant products can help an area grow.

How Plant Products Help an Area Grow

An area has plants that can be made into products that people want.

↓

_____

_____

_____

↓

_____

_____

_____

Take It Home!

Family Members: Take your child on a scavenger hunt around your home. Work together to identify products that come from natural resources.

How It's Made

Cotton Shirt

A cotton shirt is made from cotton plants. It takes many steps to make cotton into a shirt.

Raw cotton is picked and cleaned.

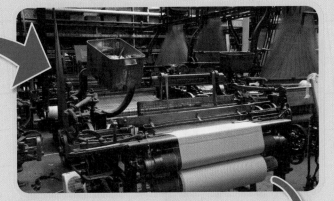

The cotton is spun into thread. The thread is woven into fabric.

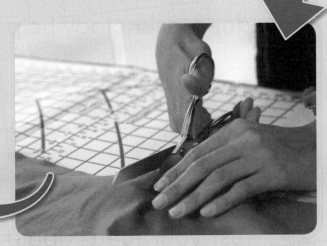

The fabric is cut into pieces. The pieces are sewn together.

S.T.E.M. continued

Out of Order

Write 1 to 4 to show the correct order of steps for making a cotton shirt. The first step is 1.

_____

_____

_____

_____

How does technology help make cotton into a shirt?

_____

_____

Build On It!

Test your ideas about building safety. Complete **Test It: Strong Buildings** on the Inquiry Flipchart.

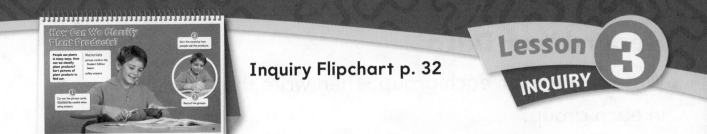

Name _____

Essential Question

How Can We Classify Plant Products?

Set a Purpose

Tell what you will do.

_____

_____

Think About the Procedure

1 How will you know which products belong in the same group?

_____

_____

2 How will you record the groups you made?

_____

_____

Record Your Data

Write a name for each group. Then write the products in each group.

Group 1	Group 2	Group 3
_____	_____	_____

Draw Conclusions

What are some kinds of products that people make from plants?

_____

_____

Ask More Questions

What other questions can you ask about plant products?

_____

_____

256

Picture Cards

Cut the cards along the dashed lines.

peanut butter

cotton shirt

wood table

straw hat

grape jelly

seagrass slippers

cotton blankets

maple syrup

corn cereal

Unit 6 Review

Vocabulary Review

Use the terms in the box to complete the sentences.

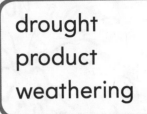

drought
product
weathering

1. When wind and water break down rock into smaller pieces, the process is called _____.

2. A long period of time with very little rain is called a _____.

3. Something made by people or machines for people to use is a _____.

Science Concepts

Fill in the letter of the choice that best answers the question.

4. Which is a slow Earth change?
   Ⓐ an earthquake
   Ⓑ erosion
   Ⓒ a flood

5. Which is a natural resource?
   Ⓐ clothes
   Ⓑ houses
   Ⓒ rocks

6. This picture shows an Earth change.

What kind of Earth change does it show?

Ⓐ an earthquake

Ⓑ erosion

Ⓒ a volcano erupting

7. What are natural resources?

Ⓐ things people cannot live without

Ⓑ things people make to protect nature

Ⓒ things from nature that people can use

8. What kind of Earth change can plants help stop?

Ⓐ erosion

Ⓑ a fire

Ⓒ a volcano

9. Which product comes from trees?

Ⓐ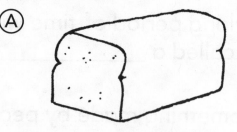

Ⓑ

Ⓒ

10. About how long could a drought last?
   Ⓐ a few minutes
   Ⓑ a few days
   Ⓒ a few months

11. Look at this natural resource.

How can people use this resource?
   Ⓐ to cook
   Ⓑ to grow plants
   Ⓒ to make buildings

12. What happens when rivers, lakes, and streams get too full?
   Ⓐ a flood
   Ⓑ an eruption from a volcano
   Ⓒ weathering

13. Which action below is a fast Earth change?
   Ⓐ Earth shakes.
   Ⓑ Land dries out over time.
   Ⓒ Stone turns to sand.

Inquiry and the Big Idea
Write the answers to these questions.

14. Look at this picture.

a. Why are these objects a natural resource?

_____

_____

b. Name two products that can be made from this resource.

_____

c. How does this natural resource help stop erosion?

_____

_____

© Houghton Mifflin Harcourt Publishing Company (bg) © Getty Images Royalty Free; (border) ©NDisc/Age Fotostock

UNIT 7
All About Weather

tornado

Big Idea

Weather changes
from day to day.

I Wonder Why
**People keep extra food and other
supplies in case of a storm. Why?**
Turn the page to find out.

Here's Why People keep extra supplies in case the power goes out and the stores are closed.

In this unit, you will explore this Big Idea, the Essential Questions, and the Investigations on the Inquiry Flipchart.

Levels of Inquiry Key ■ DIRECTED ■ GUIDED ■ INDEPENDENT

Track Your Progress

Big Idea Weather changes from day to day.

Essential Questions

Lesson 1 How Does Weather Change? 265
Inquiry Flipchart p. 33—Weather Journal/Wind Watching

Inquiry Lesson 2 How Does the Sun Heat Earth? 275
Inquiry Flipchart p. 34—How Does the Sun Heat Earth?

Lesson 3 What Are Some Weather Patterns? 277
Inquiry Flipchart p. 35—Take My Temperature/Highs and Lows

Inquiry Lesson 4 How Can We Measure Precipitation? 287
Inquiry Flipchart p. 36—How Can We Measure Precipitation?

Lesson 5 How Do Seasons Affect Living Things? 289
Inquiry Flipchart p. 37—Can You See Me?/Seasons Survey

S.T.E.M. Engineering and Technology: Watching Weather 299
Inquiry Flipchart p. 38—Improvise It: Weather Station

Lesson 6 How Can We Prepare for Severe Weather? . . 301
Inquiry Flipchart p. 39—Make Your Own Tornado/Keep It Safe!

Careers in Science: Storm Chaser 309

Unit 7 Review 311

Now I Get the Big Idea!

Science Notebook

Before you begin each lesson, be sure to write your thoughts about the Essential Question.

Essential Question

How Does Weather Change?

Engage Your Brain!

Find the answer to the question in the lesson.

What kind of weather do these clouds bring?

_____

Active Reading

Lesson Vocabulary

1. Preview the lesson.

2. Write the 4 vocabulary terms here.

_____ _____

_____ _____

Wonderful Weather

Weather is what the air outside is like. Weather may be sunny, rainy, cloudy, snowy, or windy. It can be hot or cold outside. Weather can change quickly, or it can change over many days or months.

Active Reading

The main idea is the most important idea about something. Draw a line under the main idea on this page.

Some days are warm and sunny.

On some days, rain falls.

▶ Draw what the weather is like today.

In some places, the weather gets very cold. Snow may fall.

267

Send In the Clouds

A cloud is a group of tiny drops of water or ice crystals. The drops are so light that they float in the air. The water drops may get bigger and heavier. When the drops get too heavy to float, they fall as rain or snow.

Clouds are clues about how the weather may change.

Active Reading

An effect tells what happens. Draw a line under the effect of the water drops getting too heavy to float.

Cumulus clouds are white and puffy. They usually mean sunny weather.

Stratus clouds are gray and flat. They often cover the sky. Stratus clouds may bring rain or snow.

▶ Draw clouds that bring rain. Label your picture.

Cirrus clouds are high in the sky. These thin, wispy clouds usually mean sunny weather.

Cumulonimbus clouds are thunderstorm clouds. These clouds are tall and puffy.

269

Measure It!

You can use tools to measure weather.

A rain gauge measures precipitation.

Precipitation is water that falls from the sky.

Rain, snow, sleet, and hail are precipitation.

A thermometer measures temperature.

Temperature is how hot or cold something is.

Active Reading

Find the sentence that tells the meaning of **precipitation**. Draw a line under it.

Air is all around us. **Wind** is moving air that surrounds us and takes up space. A weather vane tells the direction of the wind.

This thermometer measures temperature in degrees Fahrenheit and Celsius.

A rain gauge tells how much rain falls.

Do the Math!
Measure Temperature

Use a thermometer to measure the temperature of the air in the morning and in the afternoon. Color the pictures below to show the temperatures. Write the temperatures on the lines.

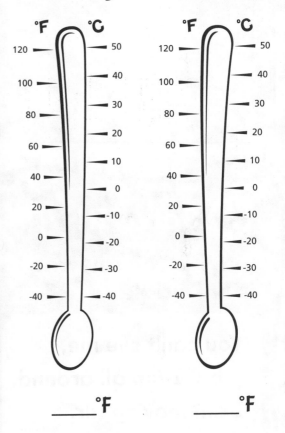

Morning   Afternoon

_____ °F   _____ °F

Write a subtraction sentence to find out how the temperature changed.

_____

Sum It Up!

1 Draw It!

Draw your favorite kind of weather.

2 Match It!

Match each tool to what it measures.

temperature

rain

3 Solve It!

Write the answer to this riddle.

You can't see me,
   but I am all around.
I am moving air.
I take up space.
   What am I?

_____

4 Order It!

Write 1, 2, 3 to order these thermometers from hottest to coldest. Use 1 for the hottest.

_____   _____   _____

Name _____

Word Play

Read the clues. Use the words to complete the puzzle.

| weather | temperature | precipitation | wind |

Across

1 What the air outside is like

2 Moving air that surrounds you and takes up space

Down

3 Water that falls as rain, snow, sleet, or hail

4 How hot or cold something is

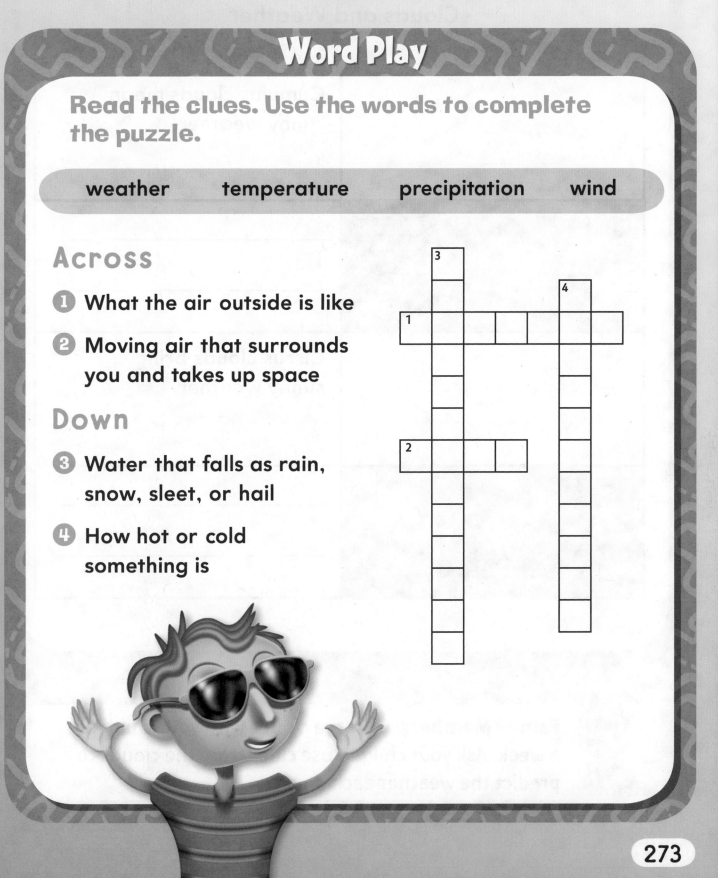

Apply Concepts

Write and draw to complete the chart.

Clouds and Weather

Clouds	Weather
	Cumulus clouds mean sunny weather.
	_____ _____
	Cirrus clouds bring sunny weather.
	_____ _____

Family Members: Observe clouds with your child for a week. Ask your child to use clues from the clouds to predict the weather each day.

Take It Home!

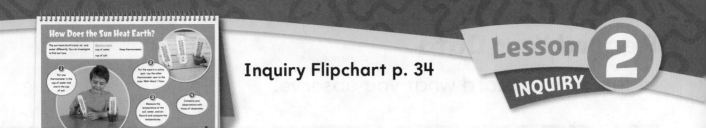

Name _____

Essential Question

How Does the Sun Heat Earth?

Set a Purpose

Write what you want to find out.

_____

_____

State Your Hypothesis

Write your hypothesis, or the statement that you will test.

_____

_____

Think About the Procedure

How will you use the thermometers?

_____

_____

Record Your Data

In this chart, record what you observe.

	Starting Temperature	Ending Temperature
air		
water		
soil		

Draw Conclusions

How does the sun heat Earth's land, air, and water differently?
How do you know?

_____

_____

_____

Ask More Questions

What other questions can you ask about the sun's heat?

_____

_____

_____

Essential Question

What Are Some Weather Patterns?

Engage Your Brain!

Find the answer to the question in the lesson.

What is the scientist doing?

The scientist is

_____.

Active Reading

Lesson Vocabulary

1. Preview the lesson.

2. Write the 4 vocabulary terms here.

_____   _____

_____   _____

A Perfect Pattern

Weather can change from hour to hour and from day to day. It changes in a pattern. A **weather pattern** is a weather change that repeats over and over.

Active Reading

Find the sentence that tells the meaning of **weather pattern**. Draw a line under the sentence.

Gentle Morning

The sun is low in the sky. It is just starting to warm Earth. The air is still cool.

Afternoon So Bright

The sun is high in the sky. It has warmed Earth and the air.

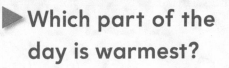

Which part of the
day is warmest?

_____

Evening Shade

The sun is setting. It no
longer warms Earth as
much. The air is cooling.

Night Fall

We cannot see the
sun. The air is cooler.
Tomorrow the pattern
will begin again.

Where Does the Water Go?

The **water cycle** is the way water moves from Earth's surface into the air and back again. The water cycle is another pattern. The water cycle causes weather to change.

Active Reading

A cause tells why something happens. What causes water to fall as precipitation? Draw one line under the cause.

The sun's heat makes water **evaporate**, or change to a gas. The gas is pushed up and meets cooler air.

Then the gas cools and condenses, or changes into tiny drops of water. The drops form clouds.

The water drops join to make bigger ones. The drops fall as precipitation.

The precipitation flows into rivers, lakes, and oceans. Then the water cycle starts again.

▶ Where will the water go when the sun heats it?

_____

_____

_____

Weather Watch

How do you know what to wear when you go outside? You think about the weather. Knowing about the weather helps people plan activities. It helps them stay safe, too.

Scientists help people find out more about weather. Scientists use tools to measure weather. Measuring weather helps scientists see patterns. Patterns help scientists predict weather. Then they can tell people what kind of weather is coming.

This weather tool measures temperature, wind speed, and precipitation.

► How do you think this weather tool helps people stay safe?

_____

_____

You can track and record weather data at home and school. Over time, the data show patterns.

	Monday	Tuesday	Wednesday	Thursday	Friday
	☀	☁	🌧	☀	☀
High	76	73	73	77	
Low	58	57	57	62	

▶ A weather report says that the day will be rainy and cold. Draw the clothes you would wear.

Sum It Up!

① Match It!

Match each picture to the word that tells about it.

morning

afternoon

② Answer It!

Fill in the blank.

What is the movement of water from Earth's surface into the air and back again called?

_____

③ Write It!

Write two reasons it is important to track weather.

_____

_____

_____

Brain Check

Name _____

Word Play

Fill in the blanks with words from the box.

| measure | evaporate | condense | water |

(1) __ __ __ __ moves in a cycle.

Heat can cause water to change to a gas, or

__ __ (2) __ __ __ __ __ (3) __ .

Scientists use tools to __ __ (4) __ __ __ __ __ weather.

Water can __ __ __ __ (5)(6) __ __ into drops.

Use the circled letters to write the answer to the question.

What do you call a weather change
that repeats over and over?

a __(1) e __(2) __(3) her p __(4) t t __(5) r __(6)

Apply Concepts

Fill in the chart. Show causes and effects in the water cycle.

Water Cycle

Cause		Effect
The sun heats water on Earth's surface.	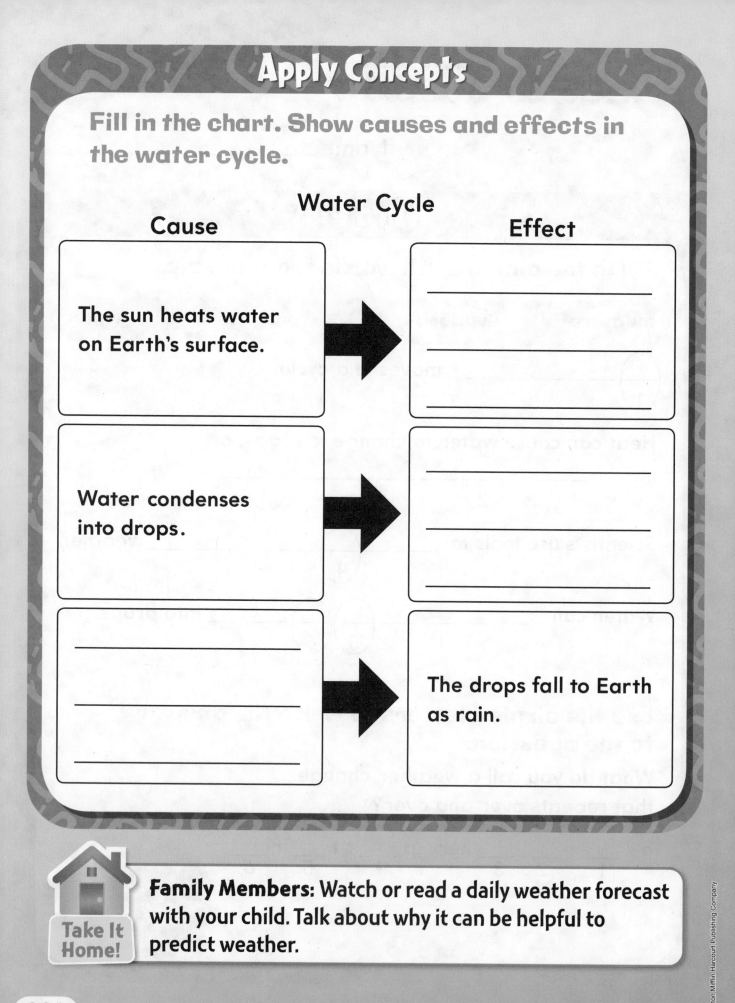	_____ _____ _____
Water condenses into drops.		_____ _____ _____
_____ _____		The drops fall to Earth as rain.

Take It Home!

Family Members: Watch or read a daily weather forecast with your child. Talk about why it can be helpful to predict weather.

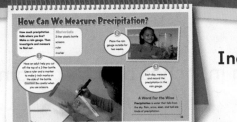
Name _____

Essential Question

How Can We Measure Precipitation?

Set a Purpose

Tell what you want to find out.

_____

Think About the Procedure

❶ Why do you make marks on the bottle?

_____

_____

❷ Why do you measure each day for two weeks?

_____

_____

_____

Record Your Data

In each box, write the day's precipitation in inches and **R** for rain, **SN** for snow, **SL** for sleet, and **H** for hail.

	Day 1	Day 2	Day 3	Day 4	Day 5	Day 6	Day 7
Week 1							
Week 2							

Draw Conclusions

On which day did the most precipitation fall? How do you know?

_____

_____

Did you observe any weather patterns? Explain.

_____

_____

Ask More Questions

What other questions could you ask about measuring weather?

_____

_____

_____

Essential Question

How Do Seasons Affect Living Things?

Engage Your Brain!

Find the answer to the question in the lesson.

When might you see ice on plants?

You might see this in

_____

Active Reading

Lesson Vocabulary

1 Preview the lesson.

2 Write the 3 vocabulary terms here.

_____   _____

_____

Season to Season

A **season** is a time of year that has a certain kind of weather. Weather changes each season. The seasons follow the same pattern every year.

Fabulous Fall

In fall the air outside may be cool. The leaves of some trees change color and drop off.

Wonderful Winter

Winter is the coldest season. Ice can form on land and plants. In some places snow may fall. Winter has the fewest hours of daylight.

▶ Which season comes after spring?

_____

Sunny Spring

In spring the air gets warmer. Some places get a lot of rain.

Super Summer

Summer is the warmest season. Some places have sudden storms. Summer has the most hours of daylight.

291

A Change of Pace

The changes in temperature and sunlight from season to season affect many living things. Plants and animals may change color. They may change what they do. Animals may change where they live.

Active Reading

A detail is a fact about a main idea. Draw one line under a detail. Draw an arrow to the main idea it tells about.

summer

fall

winter

spring

The leaves of some trees change color and drop off in fall. New leaves grow in spring.

Some animals hibernate in winter. To hibernate is to go into a deep, sleeplike state. This helps animals, like bats, save energy.

bat hibernating

The fur of the arctic fox changes color with the seasons. Look how its fur matches its environment in each season.

summer

winter

▶ Circle three ways that some living things change with the seasons.

Some animals migrate. To migrate is to travel from one place to another and back again. In fall, Canada geese fly from colder places to warmer places.

The Seasons and You

Do you wear a coat on a hot summer day? Do you swim at the beach in winter? Probably not! The seasons affect people, too. The seasons affect what we wear, how we travel, and what we do for fun.

Active Reading

The main idea is the most important idea about something. Draw two lines under the main idea.

The seasons affect the clothes you wear. You may wear cooler clothes in spring. You may wear warmer clothes in fall.

The seasons may affect how you travel. You may ride in a car or a bus in winter. You may ride your bike in summer.

The seasons affect what activities you can do.

▶ Name an activity you could do on a hot, summer day.

_____

Sum It Up!

① Match It!

Match the picture to the word that tells about it.

spring

winter

② Circle It!

Circle the ways a tree can change with the seasons.

Its leaves drop off.

It migrates.

Its leaves change color.

③ Draw It!

Draw yourself outside in your favorite season.

④ Answer It!

A gray whale swims from cold waters to warm waters in winter. What is this an example of?

_____

Word Play

Fill in the blanks. Use each word from the word bank.

| hibernate | fall | season | migrate |

Dear Aunt Lucy,

Thanks for letting me come see you. Summer is usually my favorite _____ to visit you. This time, I liked being there in _____ when the leaves were changing color.

Walking in the woods was great. It was the first time I saw birds starting to _____ to their winter homes. It was cool to learn that gophers _____.
I'll have to come in spring when they wake up!

Your nephew,

Ben

Apply Concepts

Fill in the chart. Show how seasons affect living things.

How Seasons Affect Living Things

Plants	Animals	People
_____	_____	_____
_____	_____	_____
_____	_____	_____
_____	_____	_____
_____	_____	_____
_____	_____	_____
_____	_____	_____
_____	_____	_____

Take It Home!

Family Members: Ask your child to choose a favorite season. Then discuss how changes in that season affect living things such as plants, animals, and people.

S.T.E.M.
Engineering and Technology

Watching Weather

Hurricane Airplanes

Hurricane airplanes collect data about hurricanes. The data help scientists predict and track hurricanes.

The airplane flies close to a hurricane.

Weather tools are placed in tubes. The plane drops the tubes into the hurricane.

The tubes fall into the center of the hurricane. The tools in the tubes collect storm data.

299

S.T.E.M.
continued

Weather Technology

Look at the diagram of the weather tube. Then answer the questions.

The parachute slows down the tube as it falls through the hurricane.

The tube holds weather tools. The tools collect data about wind speed and temperature.

What might happen if the parachute did not open?

_____

_____

Build On It!

Make a plan for your own weather station. Complete **Improvise It: Weather Station** on the Inquiry Flipchart.

Essential Question

How Can We Prepare for Severe Weather?

Engage Your Brain!

Find the answer to the question in the lesson.

When can wind take the shape of a cone?

when there is a

_____

Active Reading

Lesson Vocabulary

1 Preview the lesson.

2 Write the 4 vocabulary terms here.

_____   _____

_____   _____

Wild Weather

Sometimes weather gets wild! Then we have severe, or very bad, weather. A thunderstorm is one kind of severe weather. A **thunderstorm** is a storm with a lot of rain, thunder, and lightning.

Active Reading

A detail is a fact about a main idea. Draw one line under a detail. Draw an arrow to the main idea it tells about.

Lightning is a flash of electricity in the sky.

A tornado is a kind of severe weather, too. A **tornado** is a spinning cloud with a cone shape. A tornado has very strong winds.

Another kind of severe weather is a hurricane. A **hurricane** is a large storm with heavy rain and strong winds.

▶ What weather does this picture show? Label it.

_____

A hurricane can cause a lot of damage to an area.

Safety First

Storms can be dangerous. Scientists called meteorologists predict storms. They warn people about storms. Then people can do things to stay safe and be prepared for storms.

Meteorologists use tools such as computers to help predict and track severe weather.

▶ What might happen if meteorologists couldn't predict weather in your area?

_____

_____

_____

People try to protect property from severe weather.

Tips for Storm Safety

Read these tips on how to get ready for a storm. Then add your own tip at the bottom.

1. Get extra food and water.

2. Get other things you may need, such as flashlights and blankets.

3. Make a plan for your family and pets.

4. Stay inside.

5. _____

_____

_____

Sum It Up!

① Solve It!

Fill in the blank.

What kind of storm is made up of ⬤ and ⬤ ?

_____

② Draw It!

Draw yourself preparing for severe weather.

③ Circle It!

Circle the pictures that show severe weather.

 **Brain Check**

Name _____

Word Play

Find each word in the puzzle. Then answer the questions.

| thunderstorm | hurricane | lightning | tornado |

```
q  i  g  g  d  o  r  a  s  t  i  e
t  h  u  n  d  e  r  s  t  o  r  m
l  s  j  k  d  a  z  y  l  r  p  a
e  v  h  u  r  r  i  c  a  n  e  m
w  a  t  r  s  p  l  i  t  a  r  f
b  w  e  g  l  n  o  w  t  d  u  i
l  i  g  h  t  n  i  n  g  o  r  b
```

1 What might you see during a thunderstorm?

_____

2 What kind of storm always has heavy rain and strong winds?

_____

Apply Concepts

How would you prepare for severe weather in your area? Write a plan.

_____

_____

_____

_____

_____

_____

_____

_____

Take It Home!

Family Members: Work with your child to make a storm safety plan for your family.

Ask a Storm Chaser

What kinds of storms do storm chasers look for?
Most storm chasers look for tornadoes. A few storm chasers look for hurricanes.

How do you work?
Storm chasers watch the weather carefully. We learn about bad storms. We try to predict where to find them. Then we drive to see a storm.

How does storm chasing help other people?
Most storm chasers work with weather centers. If we spot a storm, we can alert the police and people on farms.

Now It's Your Turn!

▶ What question would you ask a storm chaser?

_____

_____

Safety from the Storm

▶ Draw or write the answer to each question to get to safety.

1 Your family has a storm kit. You use it if you lose power or get hurt. Draw one thing you would put in a storm kit.

2 A storm might be coming. Why should you make a plan?

3 Storm chasers spot a tornado. Draw a picture of what they might see.

4 Tornado warning! Your family follows its safety plan by finding shelter. Why?

Unit 7 Review

Vocabulary Review

Use the terms in the box to complete the sentences.

> hibernate
> precipitation
> weather
>   pattern

1. Water that falls from the sky is
   _____.

2. A weather change that
   repeats over and over is
   a _____.

3. When animals go into a deep sleeplike
   state in winter, they _____.

Science Concepts

Fill in the letter of the choice that best answers the question.

4. Which season is usually
   the warmest?

   Ⓐ spring

   Ⓑ summer

   Ⓒ winter

5. How can you prepare for
   a storm?

   Ⓐ read the temperature

   Ⓑ stand under a tree

   Ⓒ stay inside a
   safe place

6. What is the weather like in this picture?

Ⓐ cloudy and stormy

Ⓑ snowy and cold

Ⓒ sunny and hot

7. Which describes a hurricane?

Ⓐ a dark spinning cloud with a cone shape

Ⓑ a storm with rain, thunder, and lightning

Ⓒ a large storm with heavy rain and strong winds

8. You want to observe and measure how much it rains each day for two weeks. Which tool should you use?

Ⓐ a rain gauge

Ⓑ a thermometer

Ⓒ a weather vane

9. Where is air found?

Ⓐ all around us

Ⓑ only in wind

Ⓒ only in storms

10. Which tool measures the direction of wind?

Ⓐ a rain gauge

Ⓑ a thermometer

Ⓒ a weather vane

11. Which does the sun warm the most in one hour?

Ⓐ air

Ⓑ soil

Ⓒ water

12. It rained all day yesterday. Which type of cloud did you **most likely** see yesterday?

Ⓐ stratus

Ⓑ cirrus

Ⓒ cumulus

13. Look at this picture of the water cycle.

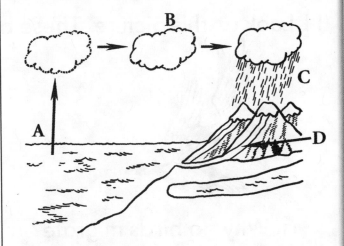

What is happening in Step C?

Ⓐ condensation

Ⓑ evaporation

Ⓒ precipitation

Inquiry and the Big Idea
Write the answers to these questions.

14. Look at this picture. These birds are migrating.

a. Why do birds migrate?

_____

b. How do your choices in clothing and activities change in winter? Name two ways.

_____

15. You observe the weather for two days and make this chart.

Our Weather				
Monday	Tuesday	Wednesday	Thursday	Friday

a. What can you conclude?

_____

b. Why is it important to track and record the weather?

_____

The Solar System

Big Idea

Earth is a planet in our solar system. Changes happen on Earth and in the sky from day to night.

a planetarium

I Wonder Why

These people are looking at the nighttime sky in a planetarium. Why? *Turn the page to find out.*

Here's Why A planetarium shows close-up pictures of faraway objects like stars and other planets.

In this unit, you will explore this Big Idea, the Essential Questions, and the Investigations on the Inquiry Flipchart.

Levels of Inquiry Key ■ DIRECTED ■ GUIDED ■ INDEPENDENT

Track Your Progress

Big Idea Earth is a planet in our solar system. Changes happen on Earth and in the sky from day to night.

Essential Questions

Lesson 1 What Are Planets and Stars? 317
Inquiry Flipchart p. 40—Seeing Stars/Go Into Orbit

People in Science: Annie Jump Cannon 327

Lesson 2 What Causes Day and Night? 329
Inquiry Flipchart p. 41—Telling Time/Shadow Changes

S.T.E.M. Engineering and Technology: Eye on the Sky 339
Inquiry Flipchart p. 42—Improvise It: Telescope

Inquiry Lesson 3 How Can We Model Day and Night? 341
Inquiry Flipchart p. 43—How Can We Model Day and Night?

Unit 8 Review 343

Now I Get the Big Idea!

Science Notebook

Before you begin each lesson, be sure to write your thoughts about the Essential Question.

Essential Question

What Are Planets and Stars?

🧠 Engage Your Brain!

Find the answer to the question in the lesson.

Name the star that Earth moves around.

_____

Active Reading

Lesson Vocabulary

1 Preview the lesson.

2 Write the 5 vocabulary terms here.

_____   _____

_____   _____

_____

All Systems Go!

We live on Earth. Earth is a planet. A **planet** is a large ball of rock or gas that moves around the sun.

The sun, the planets, and the planets' moons are parts of the **solar system**. There are eight planets in our solar system. Earth is a planet in the solar system.

sun Mercury Venus Earth Mars

▶ How many planets are in the solar system?

_____

▶ Which planet is closest to the sun?

_____

You can see some parts of the solar system only at night. During the day, the parts are still there. You just cannot see them when it is light outside.

Jupiter

Saturn

Uranus

Neptune

The planets look different. They are different sizes. They are different distances from the sun.

The Center of Attention

The sun is the center of the solar system. Earth and the other planets move in orbits around the sun. An **orbit** is the path a planet takes as it moves around the sun.

Planets closer to the sun take less time to make an orbit around the sun. Planets farther away take more time to make an orbit.

Active Reading

The main idea is the most important idea about something. Draw two lines under the main idea.

Venus

Mercury

sun

Mars

It takes one year for Earth to make one orbit around the sun.

Earth

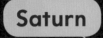

Saturn

Uranus

Neptune

▶ Why does Neptune take more time to orbit the sun than Earth takes?

_____

_____

Jupiter

Star Bright

A **star** is a huge ball of hot gases. The hot gases give off light and heat.

The star closest to Earth is the sun. You can see the sun in the daytime, but most stars can be seen only at night. They look like tiny points of light because they are so far away.

The sun gives Earth light and heat.

Some stars form constellations. A **constellation** is a group of stars that forms a pattern. What do these constellations look like to you?

Canis Major

Orion

▶ Why can you see most stars only at night?

_____

_____

Sum It Up!

1 Solve It!

Write the answer to the riddle.

I am made of planets and a sun.

I have eight planets. Suns, I have only one.

What am I?

_____

2 Draw It!

Draw Earth's orbit around the sun.

3 Match It!

Match the picture to its description.

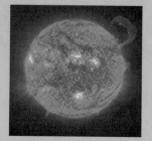

star   planet   constellation

Name _____

Word Play

Write a word from the box for each definition.

| planet | constellation | solar system | orbit |

1 a group of stars that forms a pattern ___ ___ ___ (**1**) ___ ___ ___ ___ ___ ___ ___

2 the path a planet takes as it moves around the sun ___ ___ ___ ___ ___ (**2**)

3 a large ball of rock or gas that moves around the sun ___ ___ ___ (**3**) ___ ___ ___

4 the sun, the planets, and the planets' moons

___ ___ ___ ___ (**4**) ___ ___ ___ ___ ___ ___ ___ ___ ___

Solve the riddle. Write the circled letters in order on the lines below.

I am an object in the sky that gives off light. What am I?

___ ___ ___ ___
1   2   3   4

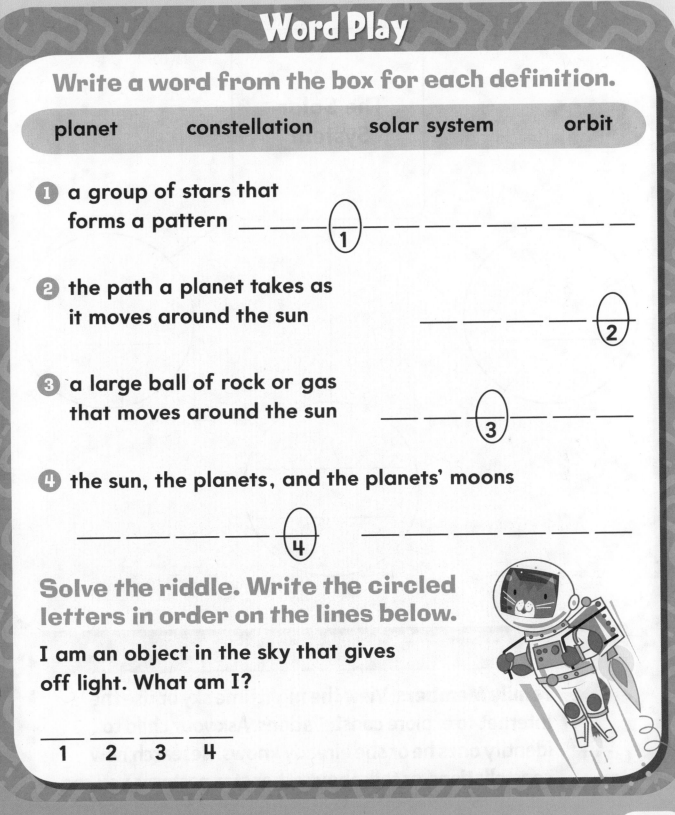

Apply Concepts

Fill in the chart. Write the parts of the solar system.

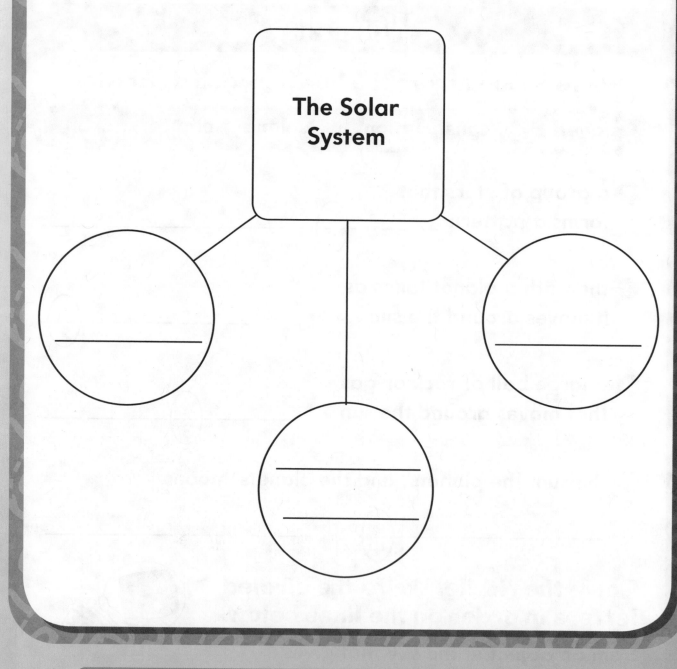

The Solar System

Family Members: View the nighttime sky or use the Internet to explore constellations. Ask your child to identify ones he or she already knows. Research new constellations, or talk about other star patterns you see.

Learn About...

Annie Jump Cannon

Growing up, Annie Jump Cannon liked to look at stars. She eventually became an astronomer. An astronomer is a scientist who studies stars, planets, and other objects in space.

Cannon studied pictures of stars. The pictures helped her sort stars into groups. Her picture groups were a new way to classify stars. Scientists still classify stars this way today.

Fun Fact

This telescope that Cannon used at the Harvard Observatory was once the largest in the country.

327

Star Power

▶ Show what you have learned about astronomers. Write the answer to each question.

1 What does an astronomer study?

2 What are some tools that astronomers use?

3 Why do you think astronomers classify stars?

4 What would you like best about being an astronomer?

1

2

3

4

Essential Question

What Causes Day and Night?

Engage Your Brain!

Find the answer to the question in the lesson.

When it is nighttime in Tokyo, it is morning where you live. Why?

Earth rotates, which causes

_____ .

Active Reading

Lesson Vocabulary

1 Preview the lesson.

2 Write the vocabulary term here.

_____

Turn, Turn, Turn

The sun seems to rise and set each day. Why? The sun does not really move. Earth is moving.

Earth turns. It takes 24 hours for Earth to **rotate**, or make one complete turn. Sunrise and sunset take place because Earth rotates.

Active Reading

A cause tells why something happens. Draw one line under a cause.

One rotation, or turn, of Earth takes one day.

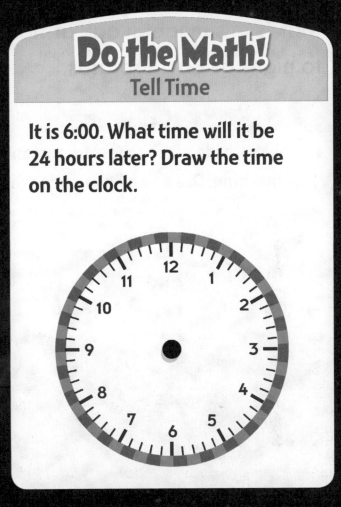

Do the Math!
Tell Time

It is 6:00. What time will it be 24 hours later? Draw the time on the clock.

Day and Night

Earth's rotation causes day and night. Look at the pictures. Find the place on Earth that is in sunlight. Look at how day changes to night as Earth rotates.

Active Reading

The main idea is the most important idea about something. Draw two lines under the main idea.

Sunlight shines on the part of Earth facing the sun. This part of Earth has daytime.

day

▶ Mark an X on the part of Earth where it is nighttime.

It is daytime where Earth faces toward the sun. It is nighttime where Earth faces away from the sun. Places on Earth move in and out of the sunlight as Earth rotates. This change causes day and night.

The part of Earth facing away from the sun is dark. This part of Earth has nighttime.

night

▶ Mark an X on the part of Earth where it is daytime.

Cast a Shadow

The sun seems to move across the sky as Earth rotates. Sunlight shines on objects from different directions as the day goes on. This causes the size, shape, and position of shadows to change.

morning

noon

Shadows are long when the sun is low in the sky. They are shorter when the sun is high in the sky. Look at the pictures to see how a shadow changes.

▶ Look at the size, shape, and position of the shadows in the pictures. Draw the shadow for early evening.

afternoon

early evening

Sum It Up!

① Circle It!

How long does it take Earth to rotate one time?

24 minutes

24 hours

24 days

② Write It!

Why does Earth have day and night?

_____

_____

_____

③ Draw It!

Draw the umbrella's shadow at different times of day.

morning

noon

336

Brain Check

Name _____

Word Play

Write a word from the word bank to complete each sentence.

| Earth | rotate | nighttime | shadow | daytime |

1. The part of Earth facing the sun has

   _____.

2. It takes 24 hours for Earth to _____ one time.

3. The size, shape, and position of a _____ changes as sunlight shines from different directions.

4. The part of Earth facing away from the sun has

   _____.

5. There is day and night because _____ rotates.

Fill in the chart. Write the effects of Earth's rotation.

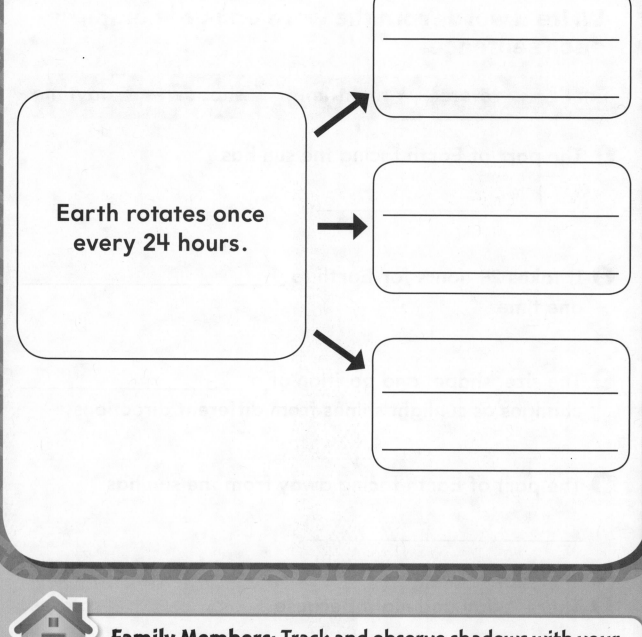

Earth rotates once every 24 hours.

© Houghton Mifflin Harcourt Publishing Company

Family Members: Track and observe shadows with your child throughout the day. Ask your child why the shadows change in size, shape, and position.

Take It Home!

Eye on the Sky

Telescopes

A telescope is a tool that makes faraway objects look larger. It helps people see the details of stars, planets, and other faraway objects.

In 1609, the astronomer Galileo invented a new telescope. He used the telescope to study space.

Telescopes today have more parts than the first telescopes had. They are made out of different materials, too.

Telescope Timeline

The telescope has changed since 1609. What do you think the telescope will look like in 50 years? Draw your idea.

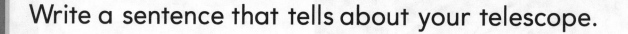

Write a sentence that tells about your telescope.

_____

_____

Build On It!

Build your own telescope. Complete **Improvise It: Telescope** on the Inquiry Flipchart.

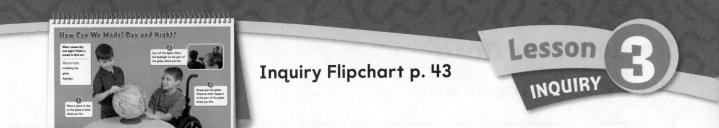

Name _____

Essential Question

How Can We Model Day and Night?

Set a Purpose

Tell what you want to do.

_____

Think About the Procedure

1 What does the globe model?

_____

2 What does the flashlight model?

_____

_____

3 Why do you have to spin the globe?

_____

_____

Record Your Data

Write what you observe.

What does the model show when the place you live is in the light?	
What does the model show when the place you live is in the dark?	

Draw Conclusions

Why does Earth have daytime and nighttime?

_____

_____

_____

Ask More Questions

What other questions could you ask about day and night?

_____

_____

_____

Unit 8 Review

Vocabulary Review

Use the terms in the box to complete the sentences.

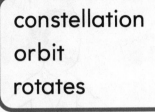

constellation
orbit
rotates

1. When a planet spins all the way around, it _____.

2. A group of stars that forms a pattern is called a(n) _____.

3. The path of a planet around the sun is a(n) _____.

Science Concepts

Fill in the letter of the choice that best answers the question.

4. Which kind of object is Earth?
   - Ⓐ a moon
   - Ⓑ a planet
   - Ⓒ a star

5. What causes day and night?
   - Ⓐ Earth's rotation
   - Ⓑ the moon's orbit
   - Ⓒ the sun rising and setting

6. Look at the girl's shadow.

What happens to her shadow as the day goes from early morning to noon?

Ⓐ Her shadow does not change.

Ⓑ Her shadow changes position only.

Ⓒ Her shadow gets shorter and changes position.

7. Which describes motion in the solar system?

Ⓐ Earth orbits around the other planets.

Ⓑ The planets orbit around the sun.

Ⓒ The sun orbits around the moon.

8. What object is shown below?

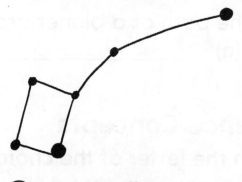

Ⓐ a constellation

Ⓑ a moon

Ⓒ a star

9. What is true about the sun?

   Ⓐ It is part of a constellation.

   Ⓑ It is the closest star to Earth.

   Ⓒ It can be seen during the day or night.

10. Look at this umbrella and its shadow.

What time was this picture **most likely** taken?

   Ⓐ early morning

   Ⓑ early afternoon

   Ⓒ early evening

11. What kind of object is at the center of the solar system?

   Ⓐ a moon

   Ⓑ a planet

   Ⓒ a star

12. About how long does it take Earth to rotate one time?

   Ⓐ 24 hours

   Ⓑ 24 days

   Ⓒ 24 years

Inquiry and the Big Idea

Write the answers to these questions.

13. This picture shows a girl and her shadow.

a. Tell how you know that the picture was taken around noon.

_____

_____

b. Name two ways that the shadow will change as the day goes on.

_____

c. Why do shadows change throughout the day?

_____

Changes in Matter

Big Idea

Matter can have different properties. Matter can be a solid, a liquid, or a gas. Properties of matter can change.

I Wonder Why

The floaties and the swim toys all keep their different shapes. Why?
Turn the page to find out.

Here's Why Gases take the shape of their container. This makes each object look different.

In this unit, you will explore this Big Idea, the Essential Questions, and the Investigations on the Inquiry Flipchart.

Levels of Inquiry Key ■ DIRECTED ■ GUIDED ■ INDEPENDENT

Track Your Progress

Big Idea Matter can have different properties. Matter can be a solid, a liquid, or a gas. Properties of matter can change.

Essential Questions

Lesson 1 What Is Matter? 349
Inquiry Flipchart p. 44—Mass in the Balance/Property Scavenger Hunt

Inquiry Lesson 2 How Can We Compare Volumes? 361
Inquiry Flipchart p. 45—How Can We Compare Volumes?

**S.T.E.M. Engineering and Technology:
Kitchen Technology** 363
Inquiry Flipchart p. 46—Think About Process: Write a Recipe

Lesson 3 How Does Matter Change? 365
Inquiry Flipchart p. 47—Evaporate Rate/What Melts?

Inquiry Lesson 4 How Can Water Change States? 373
Inquiry Flipchart p. 48—How Can Water Change States?

People in Science: Dr. Mei-Yin Chou 375

Unit 9 Review 377

Now I Get the Big Idea!

Science Notebook

Before you begin each lesson, be sure to write your thoughts about the Essential Question.

Essential Question

What Is Matter?

Engage Your Brain!

Find the answer to the question in the lesson.

What is inside the balloon?

_____

Active Reading

Lesson Vocabulary

1. Preview the lesson.

2. Write the 8 vocabulary terms here.

_____ _____

_____ _____

_____ _____

_____ _____

Matter Matters

The girl and the objects around her are matter. **Matter** is anything that takes up space and has mass. **Mass** is the amount of matter in an object.

Matter has properties. A **property** is one part of what something is like. Some properties are color, shape, size, and texture.

Active Reading

Find the sentence that tells the meaning of **mass**. Draw a line under the sentence.

Properties of Matter

▶ Look at the objects in each row. Draw something that has the same property.

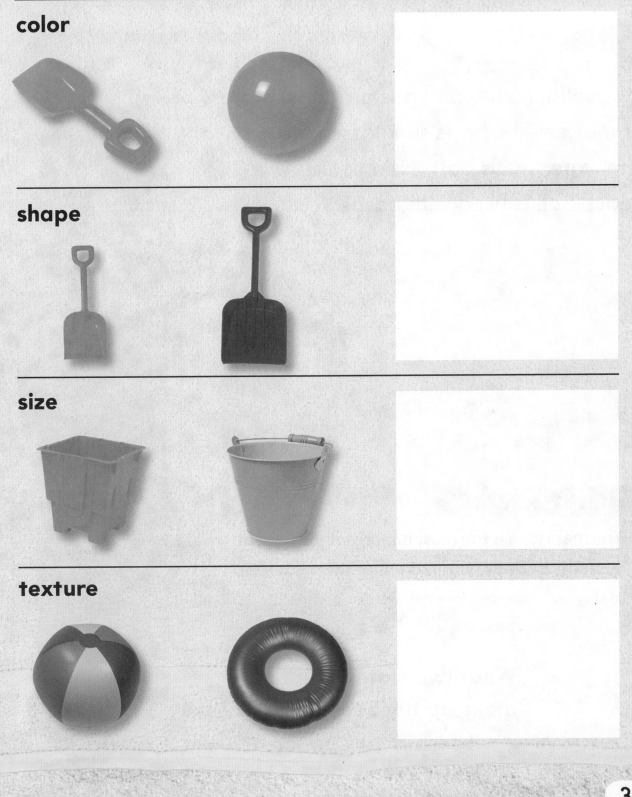

color

shape

size

texture

State of the Art

Solid, liquid, and gas are three states of matter. The boy's sunglasses are a solid. The water in his bottle is a liquid. The beach ball is filled with gases.

What two states of matter make up the beach ball?

Solid as a Rock

Look at the chair, the towel, and the hat. How are these objects the same? The answer is that all three are solids.

A **solid** is the only state of matter that has its own shape. You can measure the mass of a solid. What other solids do you see in this picture?

▶ Draw a solid object that you would take to the beach.

Shape Up!

Is juice a solid? No. It does not have its own shape. If you pour juice from a pitcher into a glass, the shape of the juice changes.

Juice is a liquid. A **liquid** is a state of matter that takes the shape of its container. You can measure the volume of a liquid. **Volume** is the amount of space that matter takes up.

▶ Compare the pitcher to the glass on its right. Which container has the larger volume?

_____

Salt water is a kind of liquid.

© Houghton Mifflin Harcourt Publishing Company (bkgd) ©Travelshots.com / Alamy

Life's a Gas

This girl is blowing air into the beach ball. Air is made up of gases. A **gas** is a state of matter that fills all the space in its container. The air will keep spreading out until it fills the entire beach ball.

Active Reading

Find the sentence that tells the meaning of **gas**. Draw a line under the sentence.

You can't see air, but you can see and feel what it does.

Wonderful Water

On the outside of this glass, water vapor is becoming liquid water.

You can't see it, but water vapor is in the air around this glass.

There are three states of water—solid, liquid, and gas. The water we drink is a liquid. Solid water is ice. Water in the form of a gas is **water vapor**.

▶ What is water vapor?

_____

_____

States of Water

Write in each empty box to complete the chart.

Name	State	Shape
ice	solid	_____
water	_____	takes the shape of its container
_____	gas	fills up all the space in a container

Sum It Up!

① Match It!

Draw lines to match each object with its state of matter.

solid

liquid

gas

② Write It!

Answer the question.

What are the three states of water?

_____

_____

_____

③ Mark It!

Sort by properties. Draw an X on the object in each group that does **not** belong.

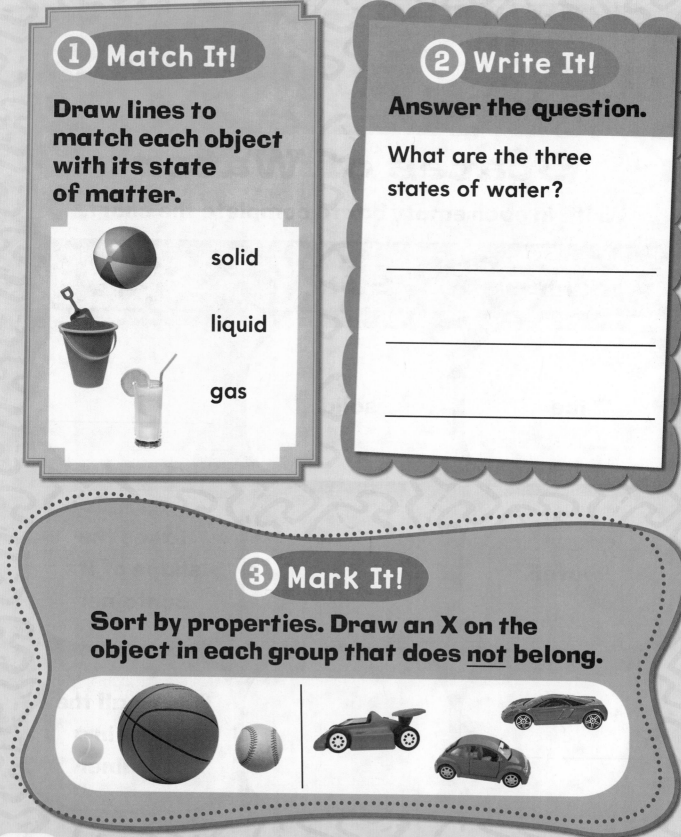

Brain Check

Name _____

Word Play

Write the word for each clue. Fill in the missing numbers in the table. Then decode the message.

a	b	c	d	e	f	g	h	i	j	k	l	m
	26	4		8	25		13		6	14		

n	o	p	q	r	s	t	u	v	w	x	y	z
7						17			10	5	12	24

takes the shape of its container

___ ___ ___ ___ ___ ___
20 23   3   2 23 16

water in the form of a gas

___ ___ ___ ___ ___
15 11   1 18 22

amount of matter in an object

___ ___ ___ ___
19 11 21 21

fills all the space of its container

___ ___ ___
 9 11 21

___ ___ ___ ___   ___ ___   ___ ___ ___
11 16 11 12   11 17   17 13   8

___ ___ ___ ___ ___   ___ ___   ___
26   8 11   4 13   23 21   11

___ ___ ___ ___ ___ ___ ___ ___   ___ ___ ___ ___ ___ ___ !
20 11   2   9 13 23   7   9   19 11 17 17   8 22

Apply Concepts

Write or draw to fill in the chart with examples of solids, liquids, and gases.

Solids, Liquids, and Gases

Solids	Liquids	Gases

Take It Home!

Family Members: Walk around your home with your child and point out objects and materials. Ask your child to classify each one as a solid, a liquid, or a gas.

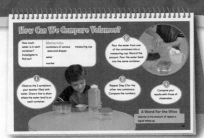
Name _____

Essential Question

How Can We Compare Volumes?

Set a Purpose

Write what you will do in this investigation.

_____

State Your Hypothesis

Write your hypothesis, or the statement that you will test.

_____

_____

Think About the Procedure

How will you figure out which container is holding the most water?

_____

_____

_____

Record Your Data

In the chart, draw the shape of each container. Write in the amount that each container held.

Shape of Container	Amount of Water

Draw Conclusions

1 How did the shape of the container affect the way you thought about which one held more water?

_____

2 How did what you thought about each container compare with the actual results?

_____

_____

Ask More Questions

What other questions can you ask about volume?

_____

_____

Kitchen Technology

Cooking Tools

The tools you use to cook are technology.
They are designed to help you in the kitchen!
A spoon is technology. So is an oven.

Whole Wheat Chocolate Chip Cookies

2 cups whole wheat flour
1 egg
1 teaspoon vanilla
1 teaspoon baking soda

A recipe tells you how to make food.

Measuring cups and spoons use standard units to measure ingredients.

A timer tells you when something has finished baking.

Make Do

Write to tell how you would solve each problem.

1. You are baking muffins. The timer on your oven is broken! How else could you measure how long to bake the muffins?

_____

_____

2. You need 3 cups of flour for a recipe. You only have a 1-cup measuring cup. How could you use it to measure the flour?

_____

_____

_____

Build On It!

Write about your favorite sandwich recipe. Complete **Think About Process: Write a Recipe** on the Inquiry Flipchart.

Essential Question

How Does Matter Change?

Engage Your Brain!

Find the answer to the question in the lesson.

How did the water turn into ice?

Water becomes ice when heat

_____.

Active Reading

Lesson Vocabulary

1 Preview the lesson.

2 Write the 2 vocabulary terms here.

_____   _____

Deep Freeze

Taking away or adding heat can change water. Think about making ice. Put water in the freezer. The water freezes into solid ice. Take the ice out of the freezer. It melts into a liquid.

Freezing changes some properties of water. Ice has its own shape. Liquid water does not. Freezing makes water expand. So ice takes up more space than water.

Active Reading

The main idea is the most important idea about something. Draw two lines under the main idea.

An ice pop is mostly water. Here it is frozen solid.

> Write the name of something that melts.

_____

_____

The ice pop gets warm and melts into a liquid.

Do the Math!
Compare Numbers

Circle the answers.

Ice cream has a lot of water in it. It melts faster when the air temperature is higher.

At which temperature will ice cream melt faster?

75 °F or 45 °F

50 °F or 85 °F

Adding and Subtracting

Adding heat can change water. Look at the water in the pot. How does the water change as the stove heats it? The water turns into water vapor. It evaporates into the air. **Evaporation** is the change of water from a liquid to a gas.

evaporation

condensation

How does water vapor change back into water? Just take away heat. Look at the water on the window. The cold window cools water vapor in the air. The water vapor changes to water. It condenses as water drops on the window. **Condensation** is the change of water from a gas to a liquid.

▶ Circle each math term that helps you understand evaporation and condensation.

Sum It Up!

① Circle It!

Circle the answer.

What happens when you heat liquid water?

evaporation

condensation

What happens when you freeze water?

It shrinks.

It expands.

② Solve It!

Write the answer to the riddle.

You see me as morning dew, or wet drops on a glass. I come around when water changes to a liquid from a gas.

What am I?

_____

③ Draw It!

Draw a solid before and after it melts.

Name _____

Word Play

Read the label in each box. Write or draw what happens to water during each change.

Changes to Water

condensation	evaporation
freezing	**melting**

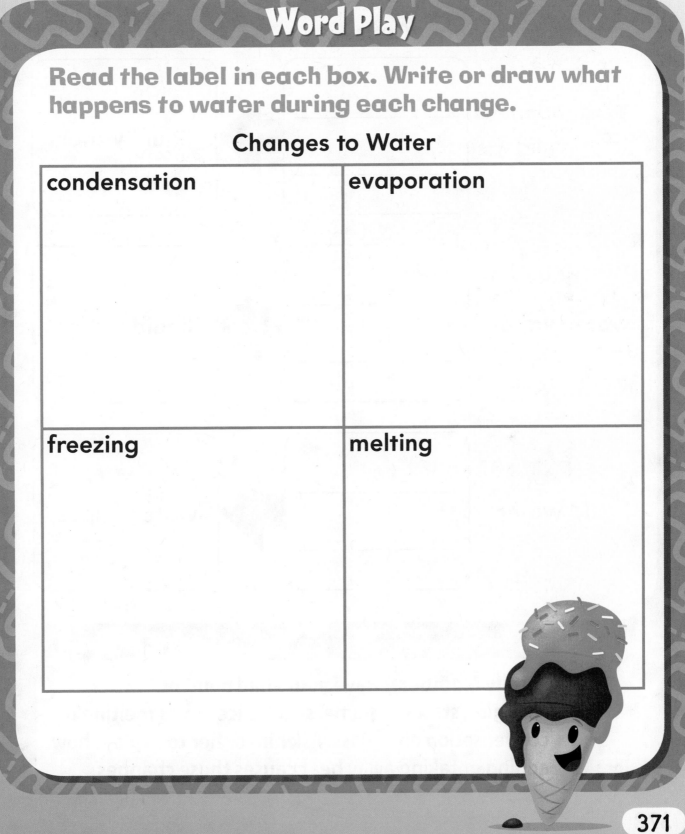

Apply Concepts

In each box, write a phrase that tells the cause of the effect.

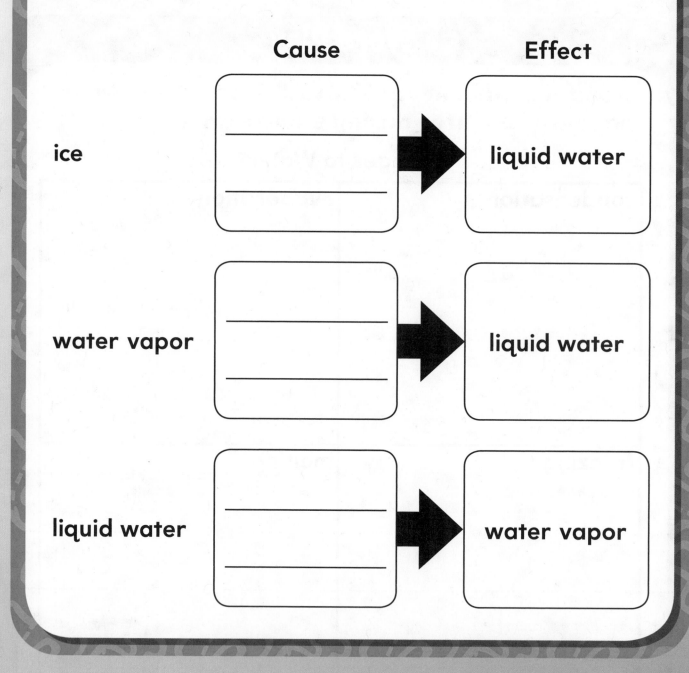

Cause		Effect
ice →		liquid water
water vapor →		liquid water
liquid water →		water vapor

Take It Home!

Family Members: Have your child point out water changing states at home, such as ice cubes melting or condensation on a glass. Ask him or her to explain how adding or taking away heat causes those changes.

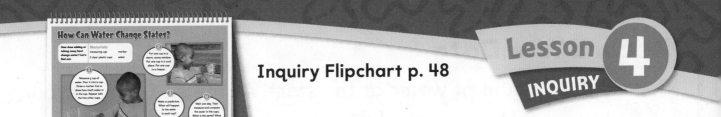

Name _____

Essential Question

How Can Water Change States?

Set a Purpose

Tell what you want to find out in this investigation.

_____

Make Predictions

What do you think will happen to the water?

_____

_____

_____

Think About the Procedure

Why do you measure the water at the beginning of the activity?
Why do you measure again at the end?

_____

_____

Record Your Data

Record the amount of water at the start. At the end, record your observations and measurements as possible.

	Warm Place	Cool Place	Freezer
Start			
End			

Draw Conclusions

Were your predictions correct? How does adding heat and taking away heat affect water?

_____

_____

_____

Ask More Questions

What other questions could you ask about the ways water can change?

_____

_____

4 Things to Know About Dr. Mei-Yin Chou

1
Dr. Chou was born in Taiwan. She studies physics. Physics is a science that tells about matter and energy.

2
She is a teacher at a university called Georgia Tech.

3
At Georgia Tech, Dr. Chou studies how gases affect solids.

4
She helps girls and women get involved in learning and teaching science.

Word Whiz

▶ **Write the words to match the clues.**

Taiwan   physics   gases   women   Georgia Tech

Across

3 Dr. Chou teaches at this university.

Down

1 Dr. Chou helps them learn about science.

2 This science tells about matter and energy.

4 Dr. Chou studies how these affect solids.

5 Dr. Chou was born in this country.

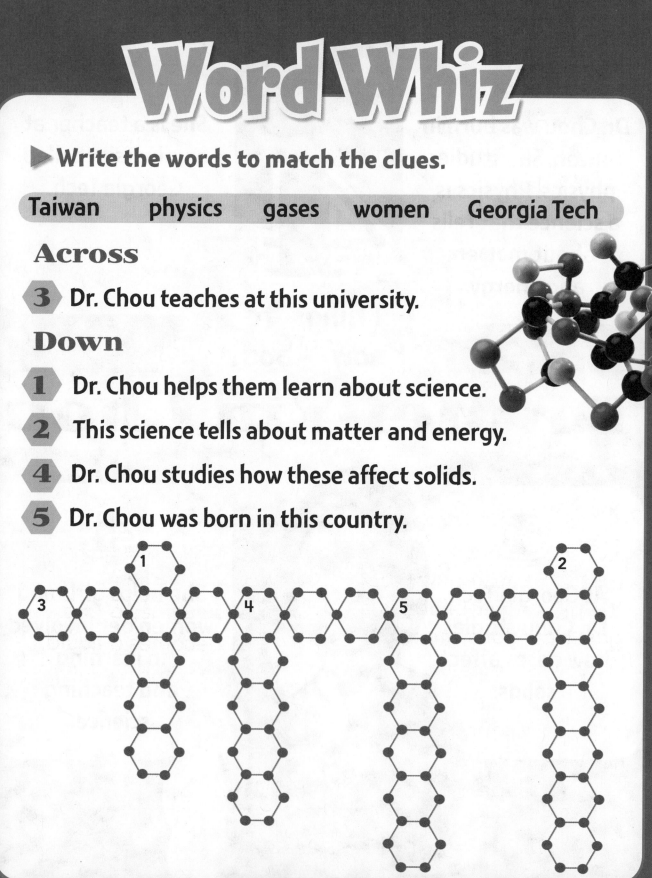

Unit 9 Review

Vocabulary Review

Use the terms in the box to complete the sentences.

> condensation
> matter
> water vapor

1. The change of water from a gas to a liquid is _____.

2. Water in the form of a gas is _____.

3. Anything that has mass and takes up space is _____.

Science Concepts

Fill in the letter of the choice that best answers the question.

4. Taylor sees a balloon filled with air. She knows that the air in the balloon is a gas. How does she know?
   - (A) The air is warm.
   - (B) The air fills all the space in the balloon.
   - (C) The air has its own shape.

5. What happens to water when it freezes?
   - (A) It becomes a gas.
   - (B) It becomes a liquid.
   - (C) It becomes a solid.

6. What is the greatest volume this measuring cup can hold?

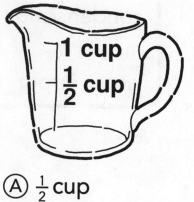

Ⓐ $\frac{1}{2}$ cup

Ⓑ 1 cup

Ⓒ 4 cups

7. Which is a solid?

Ⓐ a cloud

Ⓑ a penny

Ⓒ a puddle

8. How is the water changing?

Ⓐ It is melting.

Ⓑ It is evaporating.

Ⓒ It is condensing.

9. Which word tells the amount of space matter takes up?

Ⓐ mass

Ⓑ solid

Ⓒ volume

10. Look at the properties of this object.

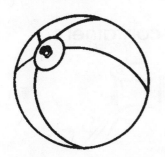

Which of these objects has about the same shape and texture?

Ⓐ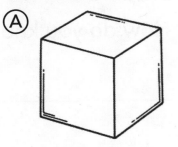

Ⓑ

Ⓒ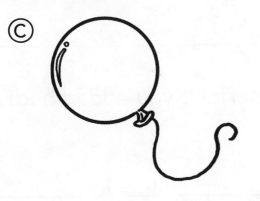

11. How does matter change when it melts?

Ⓐ It turns from a liquid to a gas.

Ⓑ It turns from a solid to a liquid.

Ⓒ It turns from a liquid to a solid.

12. Which is true about all liquids?

Ⓐ All liquids take the shape of their container.

Ⓑ All liquids have their own shape.

Ⓒ All liquids are cold.

Inquiry and the Big Idea
Write the answers to these questions.

13. The same kind of matter is in these three containers.

a. What state of matter is the material? How do you know?

_____

_____

b. How can you measure the volume of the matter in the first container?

_____

c. What would happen to the material if you added heat to it?

_____

d. What would happen to the material if you took heat away from it?

_____

Energy and Magnets

heating glass

Big Idea

Heat, light, and sound are forms of energy. Magnets attract some objects and repel others.

I Wonder Why

This man is using heat to shape the glass. Why?
Turn the page to find out.

Here's Why Adding heat to the glass causes the glass to bend. Then the man can bend the glass into the shape he wants.

In this unit, you will explore this Big Idea, the Essential Questions, and the Investigations on the Inquiry Flipchart.

Levels of Inquiry Key ■ DIRECTED ■ GUIDED ■ INDEPENDENT

Track Your Progress

Big Idea Heat, light, and sound are forms of energy. Magnets attract some objects and repel others.

Essential Questions

Lesson 1 What Is Energy? 383
Inquiry Flipchart p. 49—A Change of Light/Turn Up the Heat

People in Science: Dr. Lawnie Taylor. 395

Lesson 2 What Are Magnets? 397
Inquiry Flipchart p. 50—Action at a Distance/Magnetic Attraction

S.T.E.M. **Engineering and Technology:**
Magnets All Around 407
Inquiry Flipchart p. 51—Design It: Use Magnets

Inquiry Lesson 3 How Strong Is a Magnet? 409
Inquiry Flipchart p. 52—How Strong Is a Magnet?

Unit 10 Review 411

Now I Get the Big Idea!

Science Notebook

Before you begin each lesson, be sure to write your thoughts about the Essential Question.

Essential Question

What Is Energy?

Engage Your Brain!

Find the answer to the question in the lesson.

What kind of energy do you see in this picture?

_____ energy

Active Reading

Lesson Vocabulary

1 Preview the lesson.

2 Write the 7 vocabulary terms here.

_____ _____

_____ _____

_____ _____

_____

Full of Energy

Look at the fireworks over the city. They give off heat, light, and sound. Heat, light, and sound are kinds of energy. **Energy** is something that can cause matter to move or change.

Sound is energy you can hear.

Light is energy that lets you see. You can see objects when light shines on them. You can also see objects that give off light.

Heat is a kind of energy that makes things warmer.

▶ Circle the name of the energy that makes things warmer. Underline the name of the energy that helps you see. Draw an X on the name of the energy you can hear.

🔥 Turn Up the Heat

You can feel heat from many things. Heat from the sun warms Earth. Moving things that rub together give off heat. Rubbing your hands together warms them up. Burning fuel gives off heat. Some fuels cook food and heat homes.

Adding heat warms things. Taking away heat cools things.

The burning logs give off heat. Heat keeps the family warm.

© Houghton Mifflin Harcourt Publishing Company

The family gets cooler when the fire dies down.

► What happens when you add heat?

_____

What happens when you take heat away?

_____

See the Light

The sun, electric lights, and fire all give off light. Light is energy that lets you see. The amount of light can change how you see things.

The amount of light can change how you see the color of an object. Adding more light can make an object look brighter. Taking away light can make an object look dimmer.

How Much Light?

Different materials let different amounts of light pass through.

A window pane lets all light pass through.

A lampshade lets some light pass through.

A door lets no light pass through.

▶ Name something else that lets no light pass through.

_____

The color of the water and rocks looks dim in low light.

The color of the water and rocks looks bright in bright light.

Safe and Sound

Blow a horn. Clash cymbals. Clap your hands. What happens? You hear sound. Sound is energy you can hear.

Sound is made when an object vibrates. To **vibrate** is to move back and forth very quickly.

Active Reading

A cause tells why something happens. Draw one line under a cause.

Pitch is how high or low a sound is. Instruments have different pitches. A whistle makes a sound with a high pitch. A big drum makes a sound with a low pitch.

Cheers from a crowd are loud. Whispers are soft. **Loudness** is how loud or soft a sound is. It takes more energy to make a loud sound than a soft sound.

▶ What happens to the loudness of a sound when more energy is used to make the sound?

_____

Sum It Up!

① Write It!

Name three kinds of energy.

_____

_____

_____

② Circle It!

Circle the answer.

What happens when you add heat to something?

It gets cooler.

It gets warmer.

③ Match It!

Match each picture to the kind of energy it shows. A picture may show two kinds of energy.

  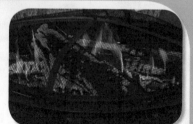

sound   heat   light

Name _____

Word Play

Write a word from the word bank for each clue.

| energy | loudness | heat | vibrate |

① how loud or soft a sound is

(1)_ _ _ _ _ _ _ _

② to move back and forth very quickly

_ (2)_ _ _ _ _

③ can cause matter to move or change

_ _ _ _ (3)_

④ energy that makes things warmer

(4)_ _ (5)_

Solve the riddle. Write the circled letters in order on the lines below.

I am energy that lets you see. What am I?

___ ___ ___ ___ ___
 1   2   3   4   5

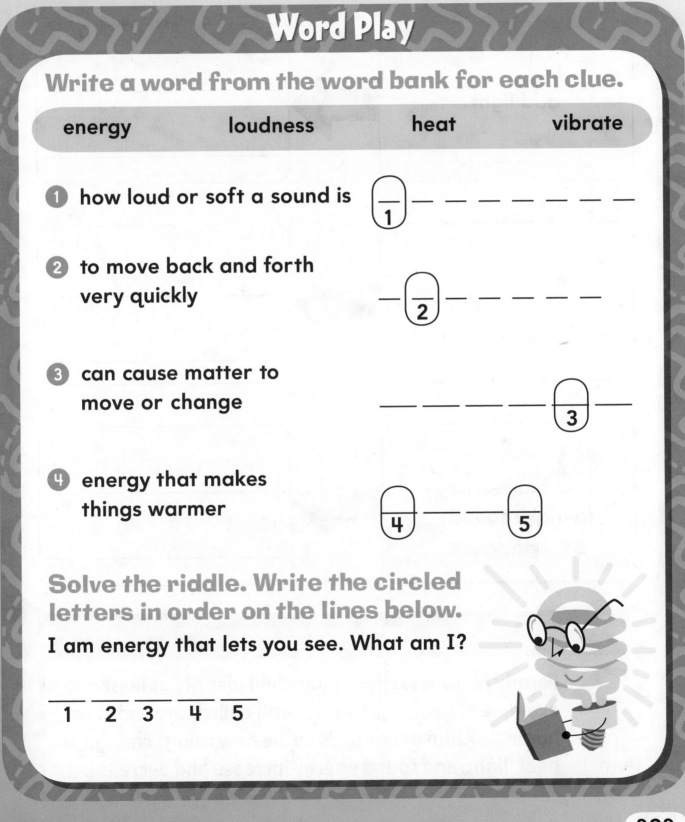

Apply Concepts

Fill in the chart. Write the effect of each cause.

Cause		Effect
add light	→	
add heat	→	
add more energy to make sound	→	

Take It Home!

Family Members: Have your child identify at least one example of heat, light, and sound energy around your home. Ask him or her to describe how things change as heat, light, and sound energy increase and decrease.

4 Things to Know About Dr. Lawnie Taylor

1 Dr. Taylor studied physics. Physics is a science that tells about matter and energy.

2 He worked for the U.S. Department of Energy for many years.

3 He studied ways to use the sun's energy to heat homes and produce electricity.

4 Dr. Taylor also studied ways to use the sun's energy to make machines run.

Let the Sun Shine!

Dr. Taylor studied solar energy. Now you can, too!

▶ Write the number of each description next to the correct picture.

1 Solar panels on a house collect the sun's energy to produce electricity or heat water.

2 A solar farm can change the sun's energy into electricity for many people to use.

3 A solar car uses the sun's energy to make it run.

▶ How have you seen solar energy used?

_____

_____

What Are Magnets?

Essential Question

🧠 Engage Your Brain!

Find the answer to the question in the lesson.

What objects are making this smiley face?

_____

Active Reading

Lesson Vocabulary

1. Preview the lesson.

2. Write the 4 vocabulary terms here.

_____ _____

_____ _____

MAGNETIC PULL

A **magnet** is an object that can pull things made of iron and steel. A magnet can push or pull other magnets.

A magnet has two poles. A **pole** is a place on a magnet where the pull is the greatest. One pole is the north-seeking, or **N**, pole. The other pole is the south-seeking, or **S**, pole.

Active Reading

Find the sentence that tells the meaning of **pole**. Draw a line under the sentence.

bar magnet

horseshoe magnet

ring magnets

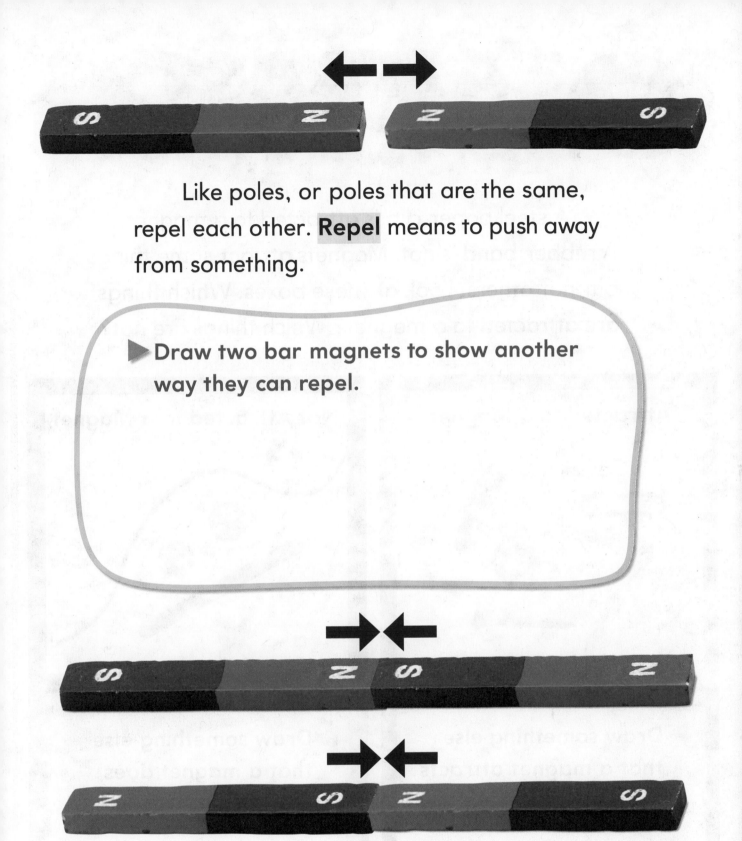

Like poles, or poles that are the same,
repel each other. **Repel** means to push away
from something.

▶ Draw two bar magnets to show another
way they can repel.

Opposite poles, or poles that are
different, attract each other. **Attract** means
to pull toward something.

ATTRACT ATTENTION

A steel paper clip is attracted to a magnet. A rubber band is not. Magnets attract some things but not others. Look at these boxes. Which things are attracted to a magnet? Which things are not?

Attracted to a Magnet

Not Attracted to a Magnet

▶ Draw something else that a magnet attracts.

▶ Draw something else that a magnet does not attract.

400

Look at the way the magnet pulls the paper clips right through the hand! A magnet does not have to touch an object to move it. This is possible because of its magnetic field. This is the area around a magnet where the magnetic force is felt.

Do the Math!
Measuring Distance

How far from a paper clip must a magnet be before it does not attract it? Use a ruler to measure.

Distance	Did the magnet attract the paper clip?
½ inch	
1 inch	
1½ inches	
2 inches	

How far from the magnet can you observe the magnetic field? How do you know?

_____

_____

MAGNETS EVERYWHERE

Magnets do much more than stick papers to the refrigerator. They help us in amazing ways! Look at the pictures to see some of the things magnets can do.

Active Reading

A detail is a fact about a main idea. Reread the captions. Draw one line under each of three details about how magnets are used.

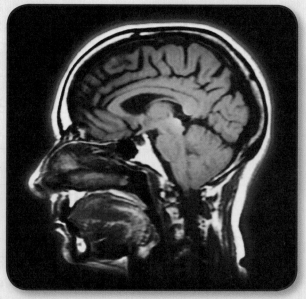

Magnets in MRI machines help make pictures of the inside of our bodies.

Huge magnets help sort items made of iron and steel before they are recycled.

▶ Draw a way you use magnets.

A Maglev train uses magnets to lift and move the train forward. One train has gone 361 miles per hour!

① Circle It!

Circle the objects a magnet attracts.

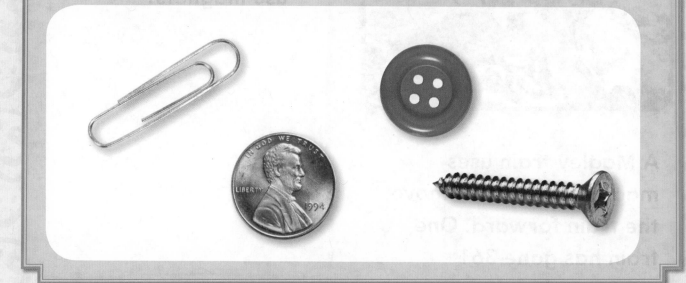

② Answer It!

Circle <u>true</u> or <u>false</u> to describe the statement.

A magnet must touch an object to attract it.

true   false

③ Draw It!

Draw a way you can use a magnet.

Word Play

Write a word from the word bank on each line to complete the friendly letter.

| magnets | poles | attract | repel |

Dear Uncle Herbie,

Thanks for the science kit! I like the

_____ the best. They make some

objects move without touching them. I used

the big magnet to _____ an iron nail.

Each magnet has two places where

the pull is the strongest. These places are

called _____. When two poles that

are the same are pointed toward each other,

they _____. They push apart really hard.

Your niece,

Olivia

Apply Concepts

Complete this graphic organizer. Write an important detail about magnets in each box.

Magnets

A magnet is an object that can push and pull other magnets and pull things made of iron and steel.

Take It Home!

Magnets All Around
Everyday Magnets

Magnets are used in many everyday things.

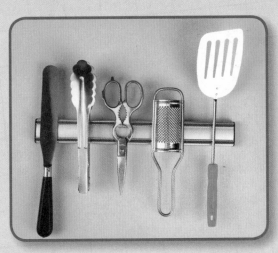

A magnet keeps these kitchen tools in order.

The magnet on this toy fishing rod attracts the metal fish to the magnet's surface.

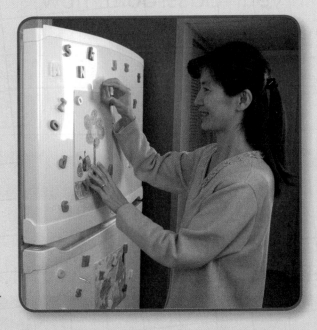

Magnets help keep the refrigerator door closed. They also attach the magnetic letters to the door.

Classroom Magnets

Draw two ways that magnets are used in your classroom.

If you did not have magnets in your classroom, how would you do the things above that you drew?

_____

_____

Build On It!

Find your own way to use magnets. Complete **Design It: Use Magnets** on the Inquiry Flipchart.

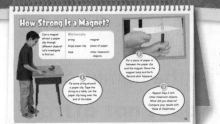
Name _____

Essential Question

How Strong Is a Magnet?

Set a Purpose

Write what you want to find out.

_____

_____

State Your Hypothesis

Write your hypothesis, or the statement that you will test.

_____

_____

Think About the Procedure

Why is it important to test the strength of the magnet with different classroom objects?

_____

_____

409

Record Your Data

Record your observations in this chart. Write the names of the three objects you tested. Circle **attracts** or **does not attract** based on your results.

Object	Attracts/Does Not Attract	
piece of paper	attracts	does not attract
object 2	attracts	does not attract
object 3	attracts	does not attract
object 4	attracts	does not attract

Draw Conclusions

1 How does putting something between the magnet and the paper clip affect the strength of the magnet?

_____

_____

2 Why do you think that happens?

_____

Ask More Questions

What other questions can you ask about magnets?

_____

Unit 10 Review

Vocabulary Review

Use the terms in the box to complete the sentences.

| energy |
| pitch |
| pole |

1. The place on a magnet where the pull is greatest is the _____.

2. Something that can cause matter to move or change is _____.

3. How high or low a sound seems is called _____.

Science Concepts

Fill in the letter of the choice that best answers the question.

4. What kind of energy results when an object vibrates?
   - Ⓐ heat
   - Ⓑ light
   - Ⓒ sound

5. What kinds of objects can a magnet attract?
   - Ⓐ all objects
   - Ⓑ only other magnets
   - Ⓒ objects made from iron or steel

6. What does this picture show about magnets?

(A) Magnets must touch objects to repel them.

(B) Magnets must touch objects to attract them.

(C) Magnets can attract objects without touching them.

7. Which are kinds of energy?

(A) heat, light, and sound

(B) heat, magnets, and light

(C) light, sound, and magnets

8. What kinds of energy does the sun give off?

(A) heat and light

(B) light and sound

(C) heat, light, and sound

9. What happens when sound energy increases?

(A) A sound vibrates.

(B) A sound gets louder.

(C) The pitch of a sound goes up.

10. Which of these objects can a magnet attract?

Ⓐ

Ⓑ

Ⓒ

11. What happens when heat is taken away from an object?
Ⓐ There is no change.
Ⓑ An object gets cooler.
Ⓒ An object gets warmer.

12. Which word tells what happens when two magnets push away from each other?
Ⓐ attract
Ⓑ pitch
Ⓒ repel

Inquiry and the Big Idea
Write the answers to these questions.

13. What are three kinds of energy? Name each kind of energy, and tell what happens to an object when you increase that kind of energy.

a. _____

b. _____

c. _____

14. Look at this object.

a. How could you move the object without touching it?

_____

b. Why is it possible to move the object that way?

_____

_____

_____

Interactive Glossary

This Interactive Glossary will help you learn how to spell and pronounce a vocabulary term. The Glossary will give you the meaning of the term. It will also show you a picture to help you understand what the term means.

Where you see **Your Turn** write your own words or draw your own picture to help you remember what the term means.

Glossary Pronunciation Key

With every glossary term, there is also a phonetic respelling. A phonetic respelling writes the word the way it sounds. This can help you pronounce new words. Use this key to help you understand the respellings.

Sound	As in	Phonetic Respelling	Sound	As in	Phonetic Respelling
a	bat	(BAT)	oh	over	(OH·ver)
ah	lock	(LAHK)	oo	pool	(POOL)
air	rare	(RAIR)	ow	out	(OWT)
ar	argue	(AR·gyoo)	oy	foil	(FOYL)
aw	law	(LAW)	s	cell	(SEL)
ay	face	(FAYS)		sit	(SIT)
ch	chapel	(CHAP·uhl)	sh	sheep	(SHEEP)
e	test	(TEST)	th	that	(THAT)
	metric	(MEH·trik)		thin	(THIN)
ee	eat	(EET)	u	pull	(PUL)
	feet	(FEET)	uh	medal	(MED·uhl)
	ski	(SKEE)		talent	(TAL·uhnt)
er	paper	(PAY·per)		pencil	(PEN·suhl)
	fern	(FERN)		onion	(UHN·yuhn)
eye	idea	(eye·DEE·uh)		playful	(PLAY·fuhl)
i	bit	(BIT)		dull	(DUHL)
ing	going	(GOH·ing)	y	yes	(YES)
k	card	(KARD)		ripe	(RYP)
	kite	(KYT)	z	bags	(BAGZ)
ngk	bank	(BANGK)	zh	treasure	(TREZH·er)

Interactive Glossary

A

adaptation (ad·uhp·TAY·shuhn)
Something that helps a living thing survive in its environment. (p. 194)

amphibian (am·FIB·ee·uhn)
The group of animals with smooth, wet skin. Young amphibians live in the water, and most adults live on land. (p. 97)

Your Turn

attract (uh·TRAKT)
To pull toward something. (p. 399)

B

basic needs (BAY·sik NEEDZ)
Certain things, such as food, water, air, and shelter, that a living thing needs to live and grow. (p. 138)

bird (BURD)
The group of animals with feathers on their bodies and wings. Most birds can fly. (p. 95)

communicate
(kuh·MYOO·ni·kayt)
To write, draw, or speak to show what you have learned. (p. 29)

condensation
(kahn·duhn·SAY·shuhn)
The process by which water vapor, a gas, changes into liquid water. (p. 369)

condense (kuhn·DENS)
To change from a gas into tiny drops of water. (p. 281)

cone (KOHN)
A part of a pine tree and some other plants where seeds form. (p. 166)

constellation
(kahn·stuh·LAY·shuhn)
A group of stars that seems to form a pattern. (p. 323)

Your Turn

Interactive Glossary

D

design process
(dih·ZYN PRAHS·es)

A set of steps that engineers follow to solve problems. (p. 45)

dinosaur (DY·nuh·sawr)

An animal that lived on Earth millions of years ago. Dinosaurs have become extinct. (p. 120)

Your Turn

draw conclusions
(DRAW kuhn·KLOO·zhuhnz)

To use information gathered during an investigation to see whether the results support the hypothesis. (p. 29)

drought (DROUT)

A long time when there is very little rain. During a drought, the land may become dry, and plants may die. (p. 231)

E

earthquake (ERTH·kwayk)
A shaking of Earth's surface.
(p. 228)

energy (EN·er·jee)
Something that can cause
matter to move or change.
(p. 384)

engineer (en·juh·NEER)
A person who uses math and
science to design technology
that solves problems. (p. 44)

environment
(en·VY·ruhn·muhnt)
All the living and nonliving
things in a place. (pp. 64, 182)

Your Turn

Interactive Glossary

erosion (uh·ROH·zhuhn)
A kind of change that happens when wind and water move rocks and soil. (p. 230)

evaporate (ee·VAP·uh·rayt)
To change from a liquid into a gas. (p. 280)

evaporation (ee·vap·uh·RAY·shuhn)
The process by which liquid water changes into water vapor, a gas. (p. 368)

extinct (ex·STINGT)
No longer existing or living. (p. 120)

Your Turn

F

fish (FISH)

The group of animals that live in water and get oxygen through gills. Fish have scales and use fins to swim and balance. (p. 98)

Your Turn

flower (FLOW·er)

The plant part that helps a plant make new plants. Part of the flower makes seeds that grow into new plants. (p. 152)

flood (FLUD)

A kind of change that happens when streams, rivers, or lakes get too full. (p. 229)

food chain (FOOD CHAYN)

A path that shows how energy moves from plants to animals. (p. 188)

Interactive Glossary

fossil (FAHS·uhl)
What is left from an animal or a plant that lived long ago. A fossil can be an imprint in a rock or bones that have turned to rock. (p. 121)

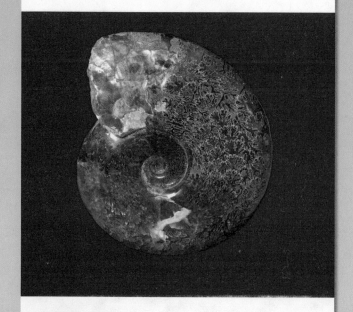

Your Turn

gas (GAS)
A state of matter that fills all the space of its container. (p. 355)

germinate (JER·muh·nayt)
To start to grow. (p. 162)

gills (GILZ)
The parts of some animals that take in oxygen from the water. (p. 83)

H

heat (HEET)
A kind of energy that makes things warmer. (p. 385)

hurricane (HER·ih·kayn)
A large storm with heavy rain and strong winds. (p. 303)

Your Turn

hibernate (HY·ber·nayt)
To go into a deep, sleeplike state for winter. (p. 293)

hypothesis (hy·PAHTH·uh·sis)
A statement that you can test. (p. 27)

The red car will roll farther because it is heavier.

Interactive Glossary

I

inquiry skills
(IN·**kwer**·ee SKILZ)
The skills people use to find
out information. (p. 4)

investigate (in·VES·tuh·gayt)
To plan and do a test to
answer a question or solve a
problem. (p. 26)

L

larva (LAHR·vuh)
Another name
for a caterpillar.
(p. 113)

insect (IN·sekt)
A kind of animal that has
three body parts and six
legs. (p. 99)

Your Turn

life cycle (LYF SY·**kuhl**)
Changes that happen to an animal or a plant during its life. (p. 107)

lightning (LYT·**ning**)
A flash of electricity in the sky. (p. 302)

Your Turn

light (LYT)
A kind of energy that lets you see. (p. 385)

liquid (LIK·**wid**)
A state of matter that takes the shape of its container. (p. 354)

Interactive Glossary

loudness (LOWD·nuhs)
How loud or soft a sound is.
(p. 391)

magnet (MAG·nit)
An object that can pull things made of iron or steel and can push or pull other magnets. (p. 398)

lungs (LUHNGZ)
The parts of humans and some animals that help them breathe by taking in oxygen from the air. (p. 82)

mammal (MAM·uhl)
The group of animals with hair or fur on their bodies. (p. 94)

Your Turn

mass (MAS)

The amount of matter in an object. (p. 350)

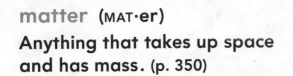

matter (MAT·er)

Anything that takes up space and has mass. (p. 350)

Your Turn

metamorphosis (met·uh·MAWR·fuh·sis)

A series of changes in appearance that some animals go through. (p. 109)

migrate (MY·grayt)

To travel from one place to another and back again. (p. 293)

Interactive Glossary

N

natural resource
(NACH·er·uhl REE·sawrs)
Anything from nature that people can use. (p. 242)

Your Turn

nutrients (NOO·tree·uhnts)
Substances that help plants grow. (p. 141)

O

orbit (AWR·bit)
The path a planet takes as it moves around the sun. Earth's orbit around the sun takes one year. (p. 320)

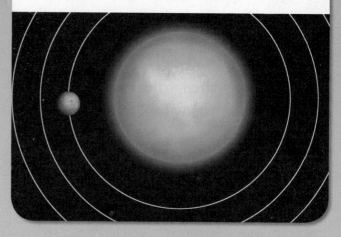

P

pitch (PICH)
How high or low a sound is. (p. 390)

planet (PLAN·it)

A large ball of rock or gas that moves around the sun. Earth is our planet. (p. 318)

Your Turn

pole (POHL)

A place on a magnet where the pull is the greatest. (p. 398)

pollen (POL·uhn)

A powder that flowers need to make seeds. Some small animals help carry pollen from one flower to another. (pp. 154, 187)

precipitation
(pri·sip·uh·TAY·shuhn)

Water that falls from the sky. Rain, snow, sleet, and hail are kinds of precipitation. (p. 270)

Interactive Glossary

product (PRAHD·uhkt)
Something made by people or machines for people to use. (p. 246)

property (PRAH·per·tee)
One part of what something is like. Color, shape, size, and texture are each a property. (p. 350)

pupa (PYOO·puh)
The part of a life cycle when a caterpillar changes into a butterfly. (p. 113)

R

repel (rih·PEL)
To push away from something. (p. 399)

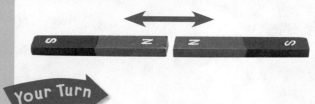

Your Turn

reproduce (ree·pruh·DOOS)
To have young, or more living things of the same kind. (p. 106)

reptile (REP·tyl)

The group of animals with dry skin covered in scales. (p. 96)

rotate (ROH·tayt)

To turn. Day and night happen when Earth rotates. (p. 330)

S

resource (REE·sawrs)

Anything people can use to meet their needs. (p. 214)

science tools (SY·uhns TOOLZ)

The tools people use to find out information. (p. 14)

Your Turn

Interactive Glossary

season (SEE·zuhn)
A time of year that has a certain kind of weather. The four seasons are spring, summer, fall, and winter. (p. 290)

Your Turn

seedling (SEED·ling)
A young plant. (p. 163)

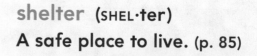

seed (SEED)
The part of a plant that new plants may grow from. (pp. 155, 160)

shelter (SHEL·ter)
A safe place to live. (p. 85)

solar system (SOH·ler SIS·tuhm)

The sun, and the planets and the planets' moons that move around the sun. (p. 318)

sound (SOWND)

Energy you can hear. (p. 384)

solid (SAHL·id)

The only state of matter that has its own shape. (p. 353)

star (STAR)

A large ball of hot gases that gives off light and heat. The sun is the closest star to Earth. (p. 322)

Interactive Glossary

survive (ser·VYV)
To stay alive. (p. 80)

technology
(tek·NOL·uh·jee)
What engineers make to meet needs and solve problems. (p. 58)

T

tadpole (TAD·pohl)
A young frog that comes out of an egg and has gills to take in oxygen from the water. (p. 108)

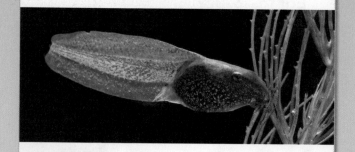

Your Turn

temperature
(TEM·per·uh·cher)
A measure of how hot or cold something is. You can measure temperature with a thermometer. (p. 270)

thermometer
(ther·MAHM·uht·ter)
A tool used to measure temperature. (p. 15)

thunderstorm
(THUHN·**der**·**stawrm**)

A storm with a lot of rain, thunder, and lightning. (p. 302)

Your Turn

tornado (tawr·**NAY**·**doh**)

A spinning cloud with a cone shape and very strong winds. (p. 303)

vibrate (**VY**·**brayt**)

To move back and forth very quickly. (p. 390)

volcano (vahl·**KAY**·**noh**)

A place where hot melted rock comes out of the ground onto Earth's surface. (p. 228)

volume (**VAHL**·**yoom**)

The amount of space that matter takes up. (p. 354)

Interactive Glossary

W

water cycle
(WAW·ter SY·kuhl)
The movement of water from Earth to the air and back again. (p. 280)

 Your Turn

water vapor
(WAW·ter VAY·per)
Water in the form of a gas. (p. 356)

weather (WEH·ther)
What the air outside is like. (p. 266)

weather pattern
(WEH·ther PAT·ern)
A weather change that
repeats over and over. (p. 278)

weathering (WEH·ther·ing)
A kind of change that
happens when wind and
water break down rock into
smaller pieces. (p. 230)

wind (WIND)
Moving air that surrounds us
and takes up space. (p. 270)

Your Turn

Index

A

Active Reading. *See* Reading Skills

adaptations
  animals, 196–197, 200–201
  plants, 194–195, 198–199

air, 82, 140

Ali, Salim, 117–118

amphibians, 97
  frog, 108–109
  newt, 97
  toad, 97

animals. *See also* amphibians; birds; fish; insects; mammals; reptiles
  adaptations, 196–197, 200–201
  antelope, 94
  bat, 187
  beaver, 212–213
  body parts of, 93
  camel, 196–197
  dog, 186
  eagle, 189
  environment and, 182–183, 212–213
  frog, 108–109
  giraffe, 197
  hibernation and migration, 293
  life cycles of, 107–113
  lion, 184
  manatee, 94
  monarch butterfly, 112–113
  as natural resources, 244
  needs of, 80–85, 182–185
  panda, 185
  plants and, 182–189
  polar bear, 110–111
  reproduction, 106
  seasons and, 293
  sea urchin, 201
  skunk, 200
  snake, 96
  tortoise, 96
  turtle, 189

Ask More Questions, 24, 36, 56, 70, 104, 130, 148, 172, 206, 256, 276, 288, 342, 362, 374, 410

astronomers, 327–328

attraction, magnetic, 399

B

balance, 16

basic needs, 138–139

birds, 95
  eagle, 189
  kiwi, 95
  owl, 184
  pelican, 95
  penguin, 196
  robin, 118
  woodpecker, 186–187

botanists, 173–174

breathing, 82–83

C

Cannon, Annie Jump, 327–328

Careers in Science
  environmental scientist, 219–220
  geologist, 239–240
  roller coaster designer, 71
  storm chaser, 309–310

Celsius, Anders, 21

Celsius scale, 21–22

Chou, Mei-Yin, 375

cirrus clouds, 269

clouds, 268–269

communicating, 29

comparing, 7

condensation, 281, 369

cones, 166–167

constellations, 323

cotton, 253–254

cumulonimbus clouds, 269

cumulus clouds, 268

D

dams, 207–208

design process, 45–51
  engineers and, 44–45

© Houghton Mifflin Harcourt Publishing Company

finding a problem, 46–47

planning and building, 48–49

testing and redesigning, 50–51

dinosaurs, 120–121

Do the Math!

compare numbers, 367

interpret a table, 83, 161

measure length, 31

measure temperature, 271

measuring distance, 401

skip count by 10s, 213

solve a problem, 60, 249

tell time, 331

Draw Conclusions, 24, 36, 56, 70, 104, 130, 148, 172, 206, 256, 276, 288, 342, 362, 374, 410

drawing conclusions, 29

drip irrigation, 145–146

drought, 231

E

Earth

changes in, 228–235

day and night, 330–333

orbit of, 320

as planet, 318

rotation of, 330–333

sun and, 330, 332–333

earthquakes, 228

energy, 384–391

heat, 385–387

light, 385, 388–389

solar, 386

sound, 384, 390–391

Engineering and Technology. *See also* **STEM (Science, Technology, Engineering, and Mathematics)**

cotton, 253–254

dams, 207–208

farms, 89–90

irrigation, 145–146

kitchen technology, 363–364

magnets, 407–408

telescopes, 339–340

weather technology, 299–300

engineers, 44–45

environment

adaptations and, 194–201

dams and, 207–208

fire and, 210–211

people and, 214–215

plants and animals, 182–183, 212–213

technology and, 64–65, 207–208

environmental scientists, 219–220

erosion, 230–233

evaporation, 280, 368

extinction, 120

F

fall season, 290

farms, 89–90

fire, 210–211

fish, 98

betta, 98

gills, 83

moorish idol, 98

shark, 98

floods, 229

flowers, 152, 154–155

food, 84

food chains, 188–189

fossils, 120–125

ammonite, 122–123

fern imprint, 121

shell, 121

Tyrannosaurus rex, 120–121

woolly mammoth, 125

freezing, 366–367

G

Galileo Galilei, 339

gases, 355

geologists, 239–240

germination, 162

gills, 83

Index

H

hand lens, 14
heat, 385–387
hibernation, 293
hurricane airplanes, 299
hurricanes, 303
hypotheses, 27

I

inferring, 9
inquiry. *See* **scientific inquiry**
Inquiry Skills
  ask more questions, 24, 36, 56, 70, 104, 130, 148, 172, 206, 256, 276, 288, 342, 362, 374, 410
  draw conclusions, 24, 36, 56, 70, 104, 130, 148, 172, 206, 256, 276, 288, 342, 362, 374, 410
  make a prediction, 205, 373
  record data, 24, 36, 56, 70, 104, 130, 148, 172, 206, 256, 276, 288, 342, 362, 374, 410
  set a purpose, 23, 35, 55, 69, 103, 129, 147, 171, 205, 255, 275, 287, 341, 361, 373, 409
  state your hypothesis, 275, 361, 409
  think about the procedure, 23, 35, 55, 69, 103, 129, 147, 171, 205, 255, 275, 287, 341, 361, 373, 409
insects, 99
  ant, 185
  beetle, 187
  butterfly, 99, 112–113
  grasshopper, 99
  ladybug, 99
  leaf insect, 201
investigations, 26
irrigation, 145–146

K

kitchen technology, 363–364

L

larva, 113
leaves, 152, 195
life cycles, 107–113, 160–167
  apple tree, 164–165
  frog, 108–109
  monarch butterfly, 112–113
  pine tree, 166–167
  polar bear, 110–111
  robin, 118
  seeds and, 160, 162–163
light, 385, 388–389
lightning, 302
liquids, 354
loudness, 391
lungs, 82

M

Maglev train, 403
magnetic field, 401
magnets, 398–403
  attraction and, 400–401
  poles of, 398–399
  uses of, 402–403, 407–408
Make a Prediction, 205, 373
mammals, 94
mass, 350, 353
matter, 350–357
  gases, 355
  liquids, 354
  properties of, 350–351
  solids, 353
  states of, 352–357, 366–369
measuring, 6
measuring cup, 15
melting, 366–367
metamorphosis, 109
migration, 293
modeling, 8
MRI machines, 402

N

natural resources, 242–249
air and water, 243
animals and plants, 244–245
economic growth and, 248–249
products and, 246–247
rocks and soil, 242
nutrients, 141

O

orbit, 320–321
oxygen, 82–83

P

people
environment and, 214–215
needs of, 80–85
seasons and, 294–295
People in Science
Ali, Salim, 117–118
Cannon, Annie Jump, 327–328
Celsius, Anders, 21
Chou, Mei-Yin, 375
Taylor, Lawnie, 395
Zavala, Maria Elena, 173
physics, 375, 395
pinecones, 166–167

pitch, 390
planets, 318–321
plants. *See also* **seeds**
adaptations, 194–195, 198–199
animals and, 182–189
cactus, 194–195, 198
daffodil, 198–199
environment and, 182–183, 212–213
flowers, 152, 154–155
kudzu, 212–213
life cycles of, 160–167
mimosa, 199
as natural resources, 245
needs of, 138–141, 182–183
nutrients and, 141
parts of, 150–155
seasons and, 292
water and, 139
water lily, 194
poles, magnetic, 398–399
pollen, 154, 187
precipitation, 270
products, 246–247
properties, 350
pupa, 113

R

rain, 270–271
rain gauge, 271
Reading Skills, 3, 4, 6, 8, 13, 15, 25, 26, 28, 43, 44, 46, 48, 57, 58, 62, 79, 80, 85, 91, 92, 94, 105, 109, 113, 119, 120, 124, 137, 138, 140, 149, 150, 154, 159, 160, 163, 164, 181, 182, 184, 186, 193, 196, 200, 209, 211, 214, 227, 228, 230, 241, 242, 244, 265, 266, 268, 270, 277, 278, 280, 289, 292, 294, 301, 302, 317, 320, 322, 329, 330, 332, 349, 350, 352, 355, 365, 366, 368, 383, 384, 386, 390, 397, 398, 402
Record Data, 24, 36, 56, 70, 104, 130, 148, 172, 206, 256, 276, 288, 342, 362, 374, 410
reproduction, 106, 187
reptiles, 96
repulsion, magnetic, 399
resources. *See* **natural resources**
roller coaster designers, 71
roots, 153
rotation, 330–333
ruler, 17

Index

S

safety
  storm, 304–305, 310
  technology and, 62–63
scale, 16
science tools, 14–17
scientific inquiry, 4–9.
  See also **Inquiry Skills**
  measuring and
    comparing, 6–7
  modeling and
    inferring, 8–9
scientific method,
  26–31
  communicating, 29
  drawing conclusions,
    29
  hypothesis, 27
  investigations, 26
  testing, 28, 30–31
seasons, 290–295
  animals and, 293
  people and, 294–295
  trees and, 292
seedlings, 163
seeds, 155
  life cycles and, 160,
    162–163
  reproduction and,
    186–187
Set a Purpose, 23, 35,
  55, 69, 103, 129, 147,
  171, 205, 255, 275,
  287, 341, 361, 373, 409
shelter, 85

solar energy, 386
solar system, 318–321
solids, 353
sound, 384, 390–391
spring season, 291
sprinkler irrigation,
  145–146
stars, 322–323, 327
State Your Hypothesis,
  275, 361, 409
**STEM (Science,
  Technology,
  Engineering, and
  Mathematics)**. *See
  also* **Engineering and
  Technology**
  Bringing Water to
    Plants, 145–146
  Eye on the Sky,
    339–340
  On the Farm, 89–90
  How It's Made: Cotton
    Shirt, 253–254
  Kitchen Technology,
    363–364
  Magnets All Around,
    407–408
  Technology and the
    Environment,
    207–208
  Watching Weather,
    299–300
stems, 153
storm chasers,
  309–310
stratus clouds, 269

summer season, 291
sun, 318, 320
  and Earth, 330,
    332–333
  shadows and, 334–335
  as star, 322
sunlight, 140
survival, 80

T

tadpoles, 108–109
tape measure, 17
Taylor, Lawnie, 395
technology, 58–65
  bathroom, 58–59
  batteries, 64–65
  environment and,
    64–65, 207–208
  home, 60–61
  kitchen, 363–364
  safety and, 62–63
  weather, 299–300
telescopes, 339–340
temperature, 21–22,
  270–271
testing, 28, 30–31
thermometers, 15,
  270–271
**Think About the
  Procedure**, 23, 35, 55,
  69, 103, 129, 147, 171,
  205, 255, 275, 287,
  341, 361, 373, 409
thunderstorms, 302
tools, measuring,
  15–17

tornadoes, 303
trees
    apple tree, 164–165
    erosion prevention by, 232–233
    pine tree, 166–167
    seasons and, 292

vibrations, 390
volcanoes, 228
volume, 354

water
    condensation, 281, 369
    evaporation, 280, 368
    irrigation, 145–146
    melting and freezing, 366–367
    plants and, 139
    states of, 356–357
    survival and, 80–81
water cycle, 280–281
water vapor, 356
weather, 266–271
    clouds, 268–269
    condensation, 281
    evaporation, 280
    hurricanes, 299–300, 303
    measuring, 270–271, 282
    patterns in, 278–279
    safety, 304–305, 310
    severe, 302–303
    temperature and, 270
    tracking and recording, 283
    water cycle, 280–281
weathering, 230
weather vanes, 270
Why It Matters, 30–31, 64–65, 82–83, 214–215, 248–249, 304–305, 402–403
wind, 270
winter season, 290

Zavala, Maria Elena, 173